Twayne's English Authors Series

Sʏʟᴠɪᴀ E. Bᴏᴡᴍᴀɴ, *Editor*

Indiana University

Samuel Pepys

Samuel Pepys

By Ivan E. Taylor

Howard University

Twayne Publishers, Inc.   ::   New York

ESTELLAE, MEAE STELLAE.

Preface

The purpose of *Samuel Pepys* is to provide for the student and general reader an account of the famous diarist's typical activities during the nine years, 1660-1669, that his *Diary* records. The *Diary* was kept in cipher on a day-to-day basis and the manuscript remained among Mr. Pepys's literary effects until it was translated in 1825 by the Reverend John Smith. Because Mr. Pepys recorded almost every activity that he performed daily, the nine-year record is a work of prodigious length; it is, therefore, more famous than it is read. In *Samuel Pepys*, I have attempted, therefore, to organize the vast material of the *Diary* to demonstrate that Mr. Pepys's average days were filled with wonderful events. The coronation of King Charles, The Plague, and the Great Fire are among the prominent events of his life; and sections of this book deal with them. Pepys did ordinary things every day, however; he went to the theater, practiced music, courted the ladies, and had the usual dealings with family and friends. Sections of the book are devoted to these affairs.

Mr. Pepys was also a remarkable average man. Starting from ordinary beginnings and the usual handicaps, he rose to power and position by diligence, design, and efficiency. Sections of this book attempt to show how Pepys climbed the social and political ladder while participating in average tasks; hence there are chapters on Mr. Pepys as politician and as schoolman and bibliophile.

There are other accounts of Mr. Pepys and his *Diary* and additional accounts will continue to be written, each extraordinary in its own way; for each deals with a remarkable book, the *Diary*. This account of Pepys is an attempt to show the man in action as he lives his average days, as each man must live his own, and to show the reader that if he would take notice of his own days he, too, would find delight, wonder, and significance in them. The book takes no liberties whatever with the facts of the *Diary*, and is careful to record the time each event happened so that the reader will be able to find the place in the actual

Diary and supply a fuller context. In a sense, therefore, this book attempts to highlight events in the *Diary* and to present them in sequential order. It is impossible to write a book, however, without putting to use my own reading, reflection, observation, and recollection. Pepys, somehow, makes one put them to use; and I have not hesitated to do so. But, then, practically no one writes a book alone. The book was written, therefore, with the aid of Mr. Samuel Pepys and with all other books on Pepys that have been written and that I have read. It provides, for practical purposes, short accounts of Mr. Pepys's life before and after the Diary; but this study is neither a biography nor a full account of the *Diary*.

Professor Sylvia Bowman of the University of Indiana has been very patient in working through what was once a manuscript of distressing length, and I am grateful to her for suggestions toward effective excision and for many other evidences of scholarly good will.

To the official family of Howard University, especially the President and Academic Deans, I am deeply grateful for bringing this book to print through grants for typing and manuscript revisions and for making it possible for me to visit Pepys-land, the narrow streets that he walked, the churches where he slept through dull sermons and, above all, the Library that bears his name at Magdalene College, Cambridge.

IVAN E. TAYLOR

Howard University

Contents

Preface

Chronology

1.	The Man and His Diary	15
2.	Politician	24
3.	Typical Days with Mr. Pepys	49
4.	A Man and His Family	62
5.	Mr. Pepys and the Ladies	81
6.	Mr. Pepys at the Coronation	88
7.	Schoolman and Bibliophile	92
8.	Mr. Pepys as Musician	101
9.	A Puritan at the Theater	112
10.	The Plague	133
11.	The Great Fire	142

Conclusion   147

Notes and References   152

Selected Bibliography   155

Index   158

Chronology

1633   Samuel Pepys born in London or Brampton, place of birth uncertain. Son of John Pepys, a London tailor, and Margaret, his wife.

1650   Entered as a sizar at Trinity Hall, Cambridge, on June 21. The *Diary* states that Pepys went to school at Huntingdon and later St. Paul's School in London, prior to 1650; also that Pepys and his brother Tom lived with a nurse, Goody Lawrence, for a time when they were children. Pepys's boyhood alternated between London and the country.

1650   Transferred to Magdalene College, Cambridge, on October 1.

1654   Graduated B.A., Magdalene College, Cambridge.

1655   Married fifteen-year-old Elizabeth St. Michel. Her father, Alexander Marchant, Sieur de St. Michel, was the son of the High Sheriff of Bauge in Anjou who disinherited him for becoming a Huguenot. His daughter, Elizabeth, brought no dowry to Samuel Pepys.

1658   Operated on for the gallstones on March 26; celebrated yearly the anniversary of the occasion of the successful operation.

1660   Accompanied Sir Edward Montagu to the Hague to restore Charles to the English throne.

1660   Appointed Clerk of the Acts of the Navy.

1660   Made M.A. by proxy at Cambridge.

1660   Sworn a Clerk of the Privy Seal.

1660   Made a justice of the peace for Middlesex, Essex, Kent, and Hampshire.

1661   Chosen a younger brother of The Trinity House (management of harbors, lighthouses, etc.).

1661   Observed the coronation of Charles II.

1661   Wrote to Duke of York on conditions at the navy office.

1661   Appointed deputy to the Earl of Sandwich.

1661   Sworn a younger brother of The Trinity House.

1662   Made a burgess of Portsmouth.

1662 Appointed a Commissioner for Tangier.

1662 Commended for his conduct by James, Duke of York.

1662 Appointed Commissioner for the Seamen's Chest (pension).

1663 Applied to be made justice of the peace in the City.

1663 Wrote a letter reproving the Earl of Sandwich for keeping a mistress.

1664 Made an assistant of the Corporation of the Royal Fishery.

1664 Questioned by King Charles on the state of the navy.

1665 Admitted to membership in the Royal Society.

1665 Appointed treasurer of Tangier.

1665 Received high commendation from the Duke of York.

1665 Called the right hand of the navy by the Duke of Albemarle.

1665 Negotiated marriage between Lady Jemimah Montagu and Mr. Philip Carteret.

1665 Removed to Woolwich because of The Plague.

1665 Appointed Surveyor General of The Victualling Office.

1666 Returned to London after The Plague.

1666 Commended by King Charles.

1666 Sat for portrait by Hales.

1666 Deputed by King Charles to help put out the Great Fire by pulling down houses; thus saved the navy office.

1666 Prepared an account for Parliament on naval expenditure.

1666 Informed the King and Privy Council concerning the bad state of the navy.

1666 Wrote a "great letter" to the Duke of York on the bad state of the navy.

1666 Applied to King Charles for money for the navy.

1667 Concerned increasingly with acquiring wealth and making it secure.

1667 Examined by committee of The House of Commons.

1668 Examined by the Commissioners of Accounts.

1668 Settled six hundred pounds as a dowry on Paulina Pepys, his sister.

1668 Summoned to attend a committee on miscarriages during the Dutch War.

1668 Defended the navy office before the House of Commons.

1668 Praised highly by Sir William Coventry and others for his defense.

1668 Spent a vacation in the west of England.

1668 Compiled a special report on the navy for the Duke of York.

1668 Lent five hundred pounds to the Earl of Sandwich.

1668 Lent five hundred pounds to Roger Pepys, M.P., his cousin.

1668 Bought a coach.

1668 Complained frequently of failing eyesight.

1669 Discontinued the *Diary*.

1669 Toured France and Holland with Mrs. Pepys.

1669 Death of wife from a fever.

1670 Engaged in unsuccessful attempt to be elected M.P. for Aldborough.

1673 Elected M.P. for Castle Rising.

1673 Appointed Secretary of the Affairs of the navy.

1677 Elected Master of the Clothworkers' Company.

1679 Accused on depositions by Colonel Scott of betraying the navy.

1679 Elected M.P. for Harwich.

1679 Committed briefly to the Tower of London.

1680 Resigned his position as Secretary for the Affairs of the Navy.

1680 Took down King Charles's narrative of his escape after the battle of Worcester.

1682 Accompanied the Duke of York to Scotland.

1682 Accompanied Lord Dartmouth to Tangier.

1684 Appointed Secretary of the Admiralty.

1684 Elected President of the Royal Society.

1685 Elected M.P. for Harwich and Sandwich.

1689 Defeated in election for M.P. for Harwich.

1690 Committed to the Gatehouse.

1690 Published "Memoirs of the Navy."

1702 Received a diploma from Oxford University.

1703 Died and was buried at St. Olave's Church, Hart Street, London.

CHAPTER 1

The Man and His Diary

THE son of an impecunious London tailor who could hardly collect his bills, Samuel Pepys had quite modest beginnings. He was probably born in London, where his father was a tailor, on February 23, 1633. Looking back across the years, he could nevertheless see in the shadows a long line of Pepises, Pepeses, and Papes going back to Edward I's time in 1273, and earlier, from whom he was descended. Simple honest men from the fenlands north of Cambridge, they had earned their living from the marshes, sometimes as freeholders of their watery acres, at other times as stywardens and hogwardens of other men's holdings. An overseer is oftentimes a better man than his lord; and, although he is seldom a bookman, he knows men. He understands how to hound his tenants, to watch them out of the corner of his eye, to tell from the smoke curling out of the chimney if they are up and about of a morning, and by the color and smell of the smoke whether they are burning green wood or have stolen a cured fence post to fry the morning's rasher of bacon. Samuel Pepys was born in London, but he went back to the fenlands every chance he had; and the hard-headed, hard-fisted ways of his ancestors were strong in him.

If Pepys had not been a Londoner by birth and circumstances, he would surely have risen to become a country overseer; in time, he would have bought or cozened his own acres; and he then would have become a substantial man, a squire, or a member of parliament. Among the wonderful circumstances in the *Diary* is the way Mr. Pepys managed to get ahead. By hard work, by mastery of the most minute details, by arising early and being the first man at his desk in the navy office, by writing things down and filing facts, by studying the failings and the good habits of other men, by anticipating the questions of his superiors and having ready answers, Mr. Pepys forged ahead in the world. Whatever had to do with the navy, he knew about it, or he made it his business to find out: planking, rope and tar, cloth for the flags, and food and beer for the sailors. Mr. Pepys came at last to be the navy purchaser. Hardly a merchant seller could cheat on quality or quantity of supplies for His Majesty's Navy, for Mr. Pepys knew all the sleights, plugged all the holes, and put affairs in order. If a merchant in a transaction did Mr. Pepys a favor, Mr. Pepys, in turn, would give him another contract. Thus by diligence, scrutiny, and circumspection, Pepys put the navy on a sound basis—and got rich.

I *The Pepys Family*

Samuel Pepys's father, John Pepys, was the son of Thomas Pepys, known as Thomas the Black to distinguish him from another brother known as Thomas the Red. Other brothers were John, Apollo, and Talbot. The last named, probably the issue of a second marriage, inherited the Manor of Impington which was bought with his mother's dowry. Samuel Pepys's father, therefore, was the youngest son of a first marriage; and, finding little prospect in the fenlands and not wanting to begin, literally, from scratch, he went down to London to seek employment. He did what tens of thousands of poor have done through the centuries: apprenticed to learn a trade, tailoring.

When the *Diary* begins, John Pepys is failing in business. He cannot collect from his customers; puts the business in the hands of one of his sons, Thomas; and returns to Brampton in August, 1661, to a small property left to Samuel Pepys by Robert, his father's brother. Samuel Pepys became the most successful son of John Pepys. Probably by survival of the fittest did he succeed, for he was the fifth of eleven children, all of whom save Thomas, Paulina, and John had died in infancy. It would indeed be poetic justice to say that Samuel started a long line of famous Pepyses; but, though the best known, he was not the only famous Pepys. Collateral Pepyses had issued other Pepyses: squires, doctors, barristers, lords of the manor, judges, bishops, and earls; for, even though it may have taken generations or even centuries to rise, hogwardens, stywardens, and pepizes became substantial Howards, Stewards, and Pepyses.

Among Samuel Pepys's forebears were the Montagus. Sir Sidney Montagu married Paulina Pepys, the half-sister of Thomas "the black" whose son John was Mr. Pepys's father. Their son,

Sir Edward Montagu was, in fact, Mr. Pepys's kinsman. Sir Edward, a navy man, had served with distinction under Oliver Cromwell, but he could obey any commander. He was chosen commander of the fleet to escort Prince Charles from Holland in 1660 to claim his English throne, for Englishmen wanted their King. Oliver Cromwell had been an efficient ruler; but, in the short two years since his death in 1658, hereditary rule under his son, Richard Cromwell, had been discredited; and trade on land and sea had become increasingly hazardous. In private conversations, in the confines of letters and diaries, in covert councils, in toasts to "the King over the water," the average Englishman, high and low, expressed his feelings: the King should return. The old commanders under Cromwell, Englishmen all, would be loyal to the chief of state. General George Monk would insure the loyalty of the soldiers; Vice Admiral Sir Edward Montagu would command the fleet of ships going to Holland to bring Prince Charles home and his brother, James, Duke of York, would become admiral of the fleet.

When Sir Edward Montagu asked kinsman Samuel Pepys to join him as his amanuensis on the voyage to Holland, Mr. Pepys agreed to go. A more nearly exact word than *secretary* is necessary to describe Samuel Pepys even at this early stage in his career, for he was a man who could get things done without having to be told to do them, and Sir Edward Montagu had noticed this trait in him. The Duke of York and Prince Charles were also to notice it. Mr. Pepys owed his being brought to the notice of the Duke of York and his quick rise to a modest plateau of success, first, to Sir Edward Montagu. When Montagu himself mismanaged his personal affairs, ran into debt and disgrace, and was sent as ambassador to Spain, Mr. Pepys had gained, by then, the confidence of the admiral, James, Duke of York, and of His Majesty King Charles.

The *Diary* years, 1660-1669, reveal not only Mr. Pepys's steady rise in influence, especially in navy affairs, but also the development of his mind and spirit. An active, inquisitive man, he was at ease in the company of virtuosos, a term which aptly describes seventeenth-century man's determination to learn how things worked, to acquire knowledge, and to own things. Mr. Pepys was a mortice and tenon man who learned to measure timber, to play on stringed instruments, to write a play or a poem, and to sing. And he could listen intently to the lectures

at the College of Virtuosos, of which he was a member and later
the president; to lectures on gross anatomy, vivisection, blood-
transfusion, the genito-urinary system, and all the mysteries of
medical science. He was an adequate linguist, a reading man,
and bibliophile who willed his library to his nephew, John Jackson, with the stipulation that it be properly housed, upon his
death, at Magdalene College of Cambridge University. The
Diary lays all these circumstances before the reader's eyes, as
well as Mr. Pepys's loving kindnesses, his honesty, and his human
frailties.

II   *Reasons for the Fame of the Diary*

Pepys's *Diary* is famous for many reasons: first, it is famous
simply by reputation, as are *Hamlet* and *Paradise Lost*. People
have heard about these works and talked about them, and they
have become household words; but the majority, perhaps, of
those who have heard and who talk have never read these works
completely. In the case of the *Diary*, it is not necessary to read
it all to sample its flavor, and a dozen entries chosen at random
may convince the unwary that he knows what is in it. In the
second place, the *Diary* is famous because of Mr. Pepys's reputation, a bad one, with the ladies. He is generally thought to
be the sexy little man, ill at ease with women of his own class
but a cad with housemaids.

If the reader goes a step farther and reads the *Diary* through,
he makes the discovery that the first reason for its fame—its reputation based on hearsay or on reading a few entries—has completely misled him. No two entries are alike, for no two of Mr.
Pepys's days were alike. Between the entry "up betimes" and
the familiar "and so to bed," his average day is crammed with
activities so diverse, momentous, and pleasurable that the ordinary man would need a week or two to sort them out and live
through them. The average man is satisfied to meet or entertain
a friend occasionally—once a day, or a week, or a year. Mr.
Pepys met crowds of men daily, and he relates in the *Diary* what
they talked about, what they planned, what they ate and drank.

Generally speaking, the *Diary* is a catalogue of little things
made to appear portentous. This fact may be still another reason
for its fame and freshness; for Mr. Pepys convinces the reader
that a catalogue of his own days could be made to appear important. And, indeed, the events of one's own daily round are of

as much prodigious and marvelous significance to one's self as a president's or a king's. Everyman feels this to be true—but Mr. Pepys has demonstrated that a man's life can be important and that any man can write the story of his days so that all men would delight in reading it. This promise may not be true in fact; but Mr. Pepys and his *Diary* beguile us to believe it. This disarming beguilement is a central reason for the fame of the *Diary*.

The *Diary* is famous, moreover, because Mr. Pepys tells a good story. Every listener or reader enjoys the narrator who edits the events of a tale, places them in sequential order, and saves a good sting for the tail of his story. A master storyteller, Mr. Pepys makes all incidents appear significant. He is in the class of Chaucer or Bunyan or the best newspaperman. The casual reader remembers, in the foregoing connection, Mr. Pepys's account of The Plague of 1665-1666, the Great Fire of London, or the Coronation of Charles, the attention to significant and personal detail: "to my great trouble hear the plague is come into the city . . . but where should it begin but in my good friend and neighbor's, Dr. Burnet, in Fenchurch Street: which in both points troubles me mightily." This is the Pepysian method of telling a story, and he is quite aware of what he is doing: The Plague is in the old city, it is close by at a neighbor's house, and the neighbor is friend and physician. He is also at his best in recording the events of the fire: "Everybody endeavoring to remove their goods, and flinging [them] into the river or bringing them into lighters that lay off [shore]; poor people staying in their houses as long as till the very fire touched them. . . . And among other things, the poor pigeons . . . were loth to leave their houses, but hovered about the windows and balconys till they were, some of them, burned, their wings, and fell down; . . ."[1]

Or, as he records the events immediately after the coronation of Charles II, he notes the details that have attended coronations time-out-of-mind to the present—details, indeed, attending the court of legendary King Arthur and found in the pages of old romance: "And the King came in with his crown on, and his sceptre in his hand, under a canopy borne up by six silver staves carried by Barons of the Cinque Ports and little bells at every end . . . and the King's first course carried up by the Knights of the Bath . . . and my Lord of Albemarle's going to the kitchen and eat a bit of the first dish that was to go to the King's table. But, above all, was these three Lords, Northumberland, and Suffolk, and the Duke of Ormond, coming before the courses on horseback, and staying so all dinner-time. . . ."[2] This passage is a mere sampling of the magnificent details of the coronation dinner presented for all time by Mr. Pepys: the awkwardness of crown and scepter at a time like this; the great lords serving as ceremonial waiters; the one testing the food for poison, who would keel over in the King's stead if there were poison. And, if the patient horses standing by had misbehaved, Mr. Pepys would have recorded the comic contretemps.

And he took sheer delight in recording unmentionable instances such as the time Lady Jemimah Montagu stopped in to visit him. Mr. Pepys, stepping from his office next door, found her sitting on the chamber pot in his dining room—and backed away in embarrassment. Or he tells of the time he was charmed by the ladies perched behind the bushes at Epsom Wells after the medicinal waters of that spa had quickly worked their way; or of the time Mr. Pepys himself rushed out of a wayside outhouse, sword in hand, to face a barking dog and, having left his belt on the toilet seat, nearly lost his breeches. The *Diary* reports a thousand such instances. Mr. Pepys, comic or serious, in big affairs and little, is a master storyteller.

Still another reason for the greatness of the *Diary,* and one close to the gift of narration, is that it contains the poetry of little things; for Mr. Pepys looks at life through the eyes of a poet. Poetry lies in his heart. The poet is the shaper not alone of verses but of events to give them life and meaning. Mr. Pepys arranges the happenings of a day in such terms that they seem to make life significant—his life and Everyman's. Poetry is a way of seeing things with the eye, but the focus of the camera lies in the heart. Mr. Pepys, so to speak, saw all things with the camera of his eye, but the focus of the lens lay within him.

Another reason for the greatness of the *Diary* is its catalogue of those pedestrian virtues that the average puritanical man fancies that he has. And English-speaking peoples, generally, are Puritans at heart; they are inheritors of the Kingdom of Heaven on earth for having earnestly coveted the best gifts set forth in the "dearly beloveds" of Archbishop Laud's Book of Common Prayer and in all the *apologiae pro vitas suas* of seventeenth-century reformers. The *Diary* is a constant reminder that there is grace abounding to the chief of sinners, grace that echoes down through the hornbooks of England and the memory gems of Isaac Watts and a thousand courtesy books down and through the admonitions of Poor Richard, telling Everyman how to conduct his affairs so that he may win that Puritan pearl of great price—getting ahead in the world.

Mr. Pepys's *Diary* is the greatest embodiment, therefore, of Puritan virtues: early to bed and early to rise makes a man . . .; a penny saved is a penny earned . . .; stay the third glass (although Mr. Pepys occasionally broke his vow and awoke next day with his head in a sad state, after vomiting all night); and mind the shop and the shop will mind you. The average man who reads the *Diary* believes that if he, like Pepys, would be faithful in business and constant in prayer, serving whatever lord or king he serves, he, too, like Pepys, could rise from a poor servant and clerk, and by sticking to his desk, could become a ruler of the King's navy, and Secretary of the Admiralty. Getting ahead was a prime virtue in Mr. Pepys, and the *Diary* shows how he did it.

Everyman sees a little, or much, of Mr. Pepys in himself; for the *Diary* is the greatest record extant of average man when unobserved by others. No man has written such an absolutely frank account of his own day-to-day conduct. Diaries, generally, are edited to show the diarist at his best or at least better than he is. No man is as good as his reputation; and, if he wants to find out what he really is, he should read the *Diary*. Everyman does not have the same faults as Mr. Pepys, but every man has his quota of faults; and, if he were as honest with himself as Mr. Pepys, he would set them down unexpurgated. And the story would be Everyman's diary.

Still another reason for the fame of the *Diary* is Mr. Pepys's friendliness and loyalty to his friends. He was at his best in the club with a circle of men. He enjoyed drinking, eating, and singing with his friends. He was also that best of friends, the good listener. Men trusted him, sought his advice, and gave him their confidence. Like many men, he was sometimes ashamed and embarrassed at the contemplation of his low-brow friends, and he was conscious of having outgrown them and of having risen above them. He always treated them well, nevertheless; and he more than compensated for any temporary lapse into snobbishness by the gracious and generous manner of treatment that he accorded those in stations even lower than those of his former friends—his own servants. This account of friendship and friendly consort, of trustworthiness, of loyalty to his inferiors, to his equals, and to his superiors lies at the heart of the *Diary*.

Close to this virtue of the art of friendship is another quality that accounts for the eternal freshness of the *Diary*: Mr. Pepys's love of life. He enjoyed the daily round. He had fun. Staying in bed with Mrs. Pepys on a Sunday morning, remaining home from church to purge himself with laxatives, pinching the girls at church, going to the alehouse, Bartholomew Fair, or the theater —always the theater. In town or in the country, Mr. Samuel Pepys enjoyed himself, went home, and recorded what he had done. The *Diary* reads like an entertainment program, a nine-year schedule of pleasures.

It is a nine-year schedule, too, of the serious struggle that England made to free its mind of error, of political lethargy, of social indifference, and of malfeasance and malfunction in high places. It is the record of the follies and moral feebleness of a good and gracious King who could not put off knighthood and put on kingship. As a result, King Charles had so many mistresses, so wasted his kingdom's substance in riotous living, and managed England with so many cabals and secret dealings that his mismanagement nearly brought her to her knees. The *Diary* records these melancholy events.

The *Diary* is a great book, moreover, because it tells the scholar, the historian, the antiquarian, and the curious reader what England was in the middle years of the seventeenth century. It would be wise, indeed, for the historian of social custom, of religion, of the church, of the theater, of the language of England, or of anything to study the *Diary*; for in it he finds on almost every page a living account of what seventeenth-century men did for a livelihood, how they entertained themselves and were entertained, how they preached and listened to sermons, how they talked, and even the very curse words that they used. Pepys, like Chaucer, Shakespeare, and Bunyan, is England's historian. One can think of a score of other books to be written on Pepys, or a hundred, on subjects like seventeenth-century preaching, reading, feeding, childbearing, medical practice, music that stirred men's hearts, dancing, the flowers that were grown, and the cultivation of the trees and orchards of England. All of these matters are revealed to the reader of the *Diary*, often in detail.

But the greatest appeal in the *Diary* lies in meeting Mr. Pepys and coming to know him and to love him: vain, self-conscious little Samuel Pepys; amorous but timid; bold-venturesome but fainthearted. Hardworking, honest, he refused to accept a handout from his inferiors, plugged up the ratholes that impoverished the King's stores, but tilted a contract his way for a gift of gold or a silver tankard. Devoted to his father, he was contemptuous of his mother and of his homely freckled sister Paulina. Standing hat-in-hand in the presence of the great ones of England, he held his own and refused to knuckle under to such as the swaggering Sir William Penn and Sir William Batten. A good man, all in all, is Samuel Pepys; and we may never have the chance to look upon the likes of him again. For there surely will never be another *Diary* like his.

CHAPTER 2

Politician

THE first entry in the *Diary* mentions the Rump[1] and Lord
Lambert[2] with restrained respect, for Mr. Pepys was not yet
the firm Royalist he came to be. Truth to tell, his political sympathies were unformed; and, if he had any convictions, they
were on the side of the Puritan-Parliament alignment. Most
Englishmen in 1658-1660 were not quite sure what kind of government they wanted. Hereditary? Richard Cromwell, inept,
had succeeded the Great Lord Protector, his father, Oliver Cromwell. Parliamentary? Roasting rumps of beef on spits in the
streets was one index of what many thought of parliament; but
the more ribald coined the epithet "kiss my rump." Military?
General George Monk,[3] commander of the armies in Scotland,
could have won power with a little fighting in the streets of
London. If a poll could have been taken (but it could not since
no one felt safe to express his views openly), the consensus
would have been, no doubt, that Prince Charles, "the king over
the water," as the drinking men symbolized him while toasting
one another over a bowl of water, should be restored to his
rightful throne.

If Mr. Samuel Pepys was unsure in his politics, he was certain
in his patron. Sir Edward Montagu, his cousin, insured his quick
rise in the world. Soon to be created Earl of Sandwich and
Knight of the Garter, Sir Edward had some rather obvious shortcomings, improvidence and wrongheadedness among them; but
history owes him a great debt. He pushed Pepys upward. He
gave him his trust, and put into his hands the management of
his household and goods, the upbringing of his children; and
he made him Pandarus in arranging their marriage: "my Lord
did begin to tell me how much he was concerned to dispose of
his children, and would have my advice and help; and propounded to match my Lady Jemimah to Sir G. Carteret's eldest son.
which I approved of, and did undertake the speaking about it

as from myself, which my Lord liked"[4] (June 23, 1665). Here is the Pepys *modus operandi* in full play: Anticipating his Lord's wishes even before His Lordship knew what his wishes and whims would be, Mr. Pepys would act as go-between and permit him to appear quite disinterested in the transaction.

Sir Edward rewarded Pepys generously by pushing him forward to fill minor vacancies, and Mr. Pepys showed his gratitude by arranging loans and signing notes for him, and by paying him the respect inherent in generally referring to him in the third person: "I called Mr. Shepley and we both went up to My Lord's lodgings at Mr. Crew's, where he bade us to go home again, and get a fire against an hour after . . . and after talking to him and me about his going to sea, he called me by myself to go along with him into the garden where he asked me how things were with me . . . He likewise bade me look out now at this turn some good place, and he would use all his own, and all the interest of his friends that he had in England to do me good. And asked me whether I could, without too much inconvenience, go to sea as his secretary . . ." (March 6, 1660). Mr. Pepys accepted the offer. His Lordship's mission was to go as Admiral of the Fleet to Holland to escort the royal princes to England and to insure His Future Majesty's safe-conduct. This secretarial assignment gave Mr. Samuel Pepys the unofficial title of Secretary to the Admiral of the Fleet, and he soon developed a technique of building a minor job to major status.

The record of the embarkation and the voyage to Holland is as fascinating as anything else in the *Diary,* but it must suffice to report that Mr. Pepys and the crew saw the Dutch shore at last on May 14, 1660. While he was ashore in Holland, Mr. Pepys's mind and character came a little more clearly into focus on May 18. He was a lover of ancient things, especially churches. The English trait of affection for old things—old monuments, old books, old letters, old trivia—was always strong in him. He visited at Delft, a few miles from the Hague, the church "where Van Trump lies entombed with a very fine monument. His epitaph concluded thus: '*Tandem Bello Anglico tantum non victor, certe invictus, vivere et vincere desiit.*' There is a sea-fight cut in marble, with the smoke, the best expressed that ever I saw in my life." Pepys visited another great church and was enraptured by the sight of the tombs, monuments, and other rarities. He was especially impressed by the sight of a poor box in every room in the houses of entertainment, and his English heart glowed at the information that every business transaction was made binding by dropping a coin therein. Each experience, so vividly re-created, is worth reliving in Mr. Pepys's company. He may even be forgiven a pun when he reports, on May 19, that upon entering a little drinking house there were a great many "Dutch boors eating of fish in boorish manner."

I *Modest Early Appointments*

The royal party returned from Holland on May 25, and Charles dispensed a regal largesse of £550 for the crew and Sir Edward's servants, Mr. Pepys included. The entry, "I spoke with the Duke of York about business, who called me Pepys by name, and upon my desire did promise me his future favour," marks the beginning of such a confident and mutually helpful association as even Mr. Pepys's nimble and fecund imagination could not possibly have encompassed. When Sir Edward Montagu advised patience and told Mr. Pepys, on June 2, that in the meantime he would do as many good turns for him as he could, he did not suggest that Mr. Pepys was an impatient, forward man; instead, Pepys always maneuvered a situation in such a way that his benefactor could take the credit for recognizing his worth. On June 6, he learned from Sir Edward that he would relinquish to Mr. Pepys his place of Clerk of the Signet if he could not find a better job for him by the end of the year.

Sir Edward Montagu soon made good his promise to find more profitable employment for Mr. Pepys, for he told him by June 18 that he had looked after the place of Clerk of the Acts for him that very day, and Pepys started promptly to enjoy the emoluments of office. The next day, he states that Captain Murford called on him and showed him five pieces to get a business done for him; and Pepys resolved to do it. He received two other gifts the same day: five pounds from Lady Pickering, who asked him to intercede with Sir Edward Montagu in her husband's case, and a quantity of chocolate from an unknown favor-seeker.

Sir Edward Montagu, meanwhile, was moving in higher circles and was proceeding adroitly toward power and position. He was made Privy Counsellor on June 21, even though cutting the red tape and pressing the outstretched palm in order to secure this honor cost him the substantial sum of twenty-six pounds.

Every man seemed to have had his hand out, and Mr. Pepys's was not the only itching palm. He records on June 21: "Captain Curle, late of the *Maria,* gave me five pieces in gold and a silver can for my wife for the commission I did give him this day for his ship, dated April 20, 1660 last."

Mr. Pepys had to hustle, however, to secure the position of Clerk of the Acts. He spoke to Mr. William Coventry, secretary to the Lord High Admiral, James, Duke of York, about the situation; and Coventry promised his assistance. When Pepys went to the Admiralty to see Mr. Thomas Turner of the navy office about the job, he discovered that General Monk's lady had written to Sir Edward Montagu on June 25 to suggest that her husband wished to assign someone to the job of Clerk of the Acts. Sir Edward had testily refused to call on her Ladyship and meeting her brother, Sir Thomas Clarges, at Whitehall, had told him that Monk certainly would take offense if he, Sir Edward Montagu, should try to name an officer to the General's army. He intended, on his part, to name this particular officer to the navy.

On the next day, June 26, even though Pepys was not officially in office as Clerk of the Acts, he accepted five pieces of gold from a merchant, Mr. Throgmorton, who made the offer over a round of drinks at the "Three Tuns" if Mr. Pepys would provide a convoy to Bilbao. What really concerned him about his new job was an offer from Mr. Watts, a merchant, to pay him five hundred pounds if he would simply relinquish all claims to it. Generally speaking, Pepys was not the kind of man to let go a bird in the hand; but he had already discovered that the perquisites of the job exceeded the pay. He would fight to keep it.

The first business of the following day, June 27, was to accompany Sir Edward Montagu to see the Lord High Admiral, James, Duke of York, who told his secretary to dispatch Mr. Pepys's business and to secure him in his position as Clerk of the Acts. Pepys was pleased that everyone congratulated him as though his position were a *fait accompli.* Although he secured a written warrant from the Duke of York to be Clerk of the Acts on June 29, real danger threatened from an unexpected quarter. He learned that a Mr. Thomas Barlow, who had held the job as Secretary of the Acts during the interregnum, was coming to town to see about it. By calling meetings, making decisions, hiring clerks, and securing written patents, Sir Edward Montagu and Mr. Pepys secured their positions, especially Mr. Pepys who moved to his navy office and lodgings in Seething Lane on July 13. The King, meanwhile, had decided to raise Sir Edward Montagu to the peerage with the titles Earl of Sandwich, Viscount Hinchingbroke, and Baron of St. Neot's; and Mr. Pepys proudly records that he dined all alone with his Lord on Sunday, July 15.

The Earl of Sandwich proved as good as his word in keeping his promise to put the new Clerk of the Acts in the way of any remunerative job that he could find. Securing such a position meant that, though the post may have been a sinecure or an unimportant one, anyone who had to ask a favor of the official who held it would leave a token of appreciation. Through the Earl's intercession, Mr. Pepys received a commission, on July 19, to swear people with the oath of allegiance. As if to reassure himself that during the interregnum he had been loyal to the King, he took Mr. and Mrs. Michell[5] and Mrs. Murford[6] to the "Dog," treated them, and over drinks reminded them—and they, him—of how they used to discuss the King privately in the time of the Rump. After all, it would not do to have it said that Commissioner Pepys, now administering the oath of allegiance, had once been lukewarm to the monarchy.

On July 21, he cautiously reminded his Lordship of the promise to secure for him the job of Clerk of the Privy Seal,[7] received a favorable answer, and was sworn in on July 23. In addition to these three positions—Clerk of the Acts, the modest commissionership of the oath of allegiance, and the month-to-month clerkship of the Privy Seal—the Earl of Sandwich had appointed Mr. Pepys to be his own secretary; and he paid him on July 30 fifty pounds for his services for the first quarter.

II Relationships with Sir William Penn and Other Navy Men

In the earlier years at the navy office, circumstances brought Mr. Pepys into closer contact with Sir William Penn than with any of the other commissioners or principal officers. His attitude toward his office-mate, Sir William Penn, was at first cautious and tentative. Pepys had a slight misunderstanding with him on August 22, 1660, when Sir William asked him to endorse Mr. Turner's petition to the Duke of York for an extra allowance to him of a clerk's salary. Mr. Pepys demurred, saying that his endorsement of such a petition might imply that he was incapable of performing his duties as Clerk of the Acts; but Sir William disavowed any such implications and satisfied him for the time being.

Sir William, nevertheless, asked him to visit on the night of September 8; and Mr. Pepys admitted that he sat late with him drinking wine and discoursing, and that he found him to be a very sociable man and able but very cunning. This sharp sense of judgment came to Mr. Pepys quite early in his career. Sir William Penn had told him on August 21 that he had been brought up and trained by Commissioner Sir William Batten, and Mr. Pepys soon learned to be extremely cautious in dealing with both; but by diligence and mastery of the details of the navy office, he eventually made himself indispensable.

The usually mild Mr. Pepys could become greatly disturbed by wrongs, real or fancied, that Penn had inflicted upon him; and on more than one occasion, even though Sir William outranked him, Mr. Pepys stood up to him. Sir William followed Mr. Pepys home to dinner on Sunday, September 9, admitting that the meal, his wife, and his household were very handsome; and this visit was not the last one; but whenever the two men swapped courtesies, Mr. Pepys lost in the deal. On October 9, on a trip to Deptford, Pepys had discovered and enjoyed a display of Sir William's merry, blunt, and bawdy disposition; but the relationship soon took a turn for the worse. Sir William Penn drank too much, talked too much, and could not take a practical joke played on himself. Mr. Pepys's disenchantment with him increased so that by Sunday, June 29, 1662, he accused Sir William of the mangy fault, among others, of fawning: "Whatever the matter is, he do much fawn upon me, and I perceive would not fall out with me, and his daughter mighty officious to my wife, but I shall never be deceived again by him, but do hate him and his traitorous tricks with all my heart. . . ." Sir William Penn's tenure at the navy office lasted until November, 1668; and the day-to-day relationship with Mr. Pepys continued brittle. Pepys thought of him as "a counterfeit rogue" and "a cheating fellow," especially when he wished of Mr. Pepys a favor of some kind involving the official records of the navy office, a bill to be paid, or a favorable chit entered; for Mr. Pepys was no man to finagle with the account books at the office.

Toward Sir William Batten Pepys's attitude was more temperate; toward William, Viscount Brouncker, appointed an extra Commissioner on December 7, 1664, he was at first cordial but later suspicious when he discovered that one of his main sources of gratuity, Sir William Warren, had enlisted Lord Brouncker's support in securing navy contracts for shipbuilding timber which Mr. Pepys alone had formerly turned into Warren's hands. Pepys snubbed both Warren and Brouncker thereafter. He learned, indeed, to pick his way around the obstacles of the Restoration course with the most skillful of them all.

III *Mr. Pepys Maneuvers with Skill*

Although he claimed ignorance of the duties of his new office, Mr. Pepys was mighty pleased with the modest title of Justice of the Peace for Middlesex, Essex, Kent, and Southampton to which he was named on September 24, 1660. Meantime, at the navy office, Mr. Pepys very skillfully and with great patience maneuvered to upgrade his position of Clerk of the Acts to that of Principal Officer, of equal rank with Sir William Penn, Sir William Batten, and others. An effective tactic that he used in achieving this elevation was devotion to duty and mastery of all the details of the office. He was probably present and at his desk more often and for longer hours than all the other principal officers together.

In a day when absenteeism and boondoggling were chronic, Mr. Pepys was usually at work, and his being there was a combination of dutifulness and design. He intended to make himself the master of Penn and Batten in particular and of all who came and went throughout the years. He would learn arithmetic from a private tutor, and all about ships from him and from any man who would explain about anything that went on water, and he would improve his own penmanship by writing fair. He would hire clerks who would be personally loyal to him, and he would insure their loyalty by dining them frequently at his house. He would spy on his office mates and slip secret reports and memoranda to the Lord High Admiral. He would, at all costs, succeed and become a good, indispensable navy commissioner. He was the youngest, the lowliest born, and the least secure; but there were ways for a man to go up in the world, and these he would learn.

Meantime, the everlasting worry of the navy office was lack

of money. Each day brought money problems. On the morning of November 10, 1660, he and Sir William Batten began to make up an account of the wages of the officers and mariners at sea to be presented to Parliament. The Treasurer of the Navy, Sir George Carteret, and the Comptroller, Colonel Robert Slingsby, joined them later that morning to assist in preparing the report. Leaving it to be written out in a fair copy, Mr. Pepys took a rough copy of the payroll to Parliament for whatever use he may have wished to make of it. Comptroller Slingsby and Mr. Pepys went to the coffeehouse where the Comptroller confided to him that His Majesty owed him six thousand pounds; and Pepys stated in the *Diary* that he did not see how this sum would be paid, since Parliament was already beginning to dispute the just sea debts. The navy pay was a constant source of trouble to the office. On occasion the sailors were restive to the stage of mutiny, and Mr. Pepys then resorted to slipping in and out of the office by way of the back door since even the sailors came to realize that the Clerk of the Acts, Mr. Pepys, was the most influential man in the navy office.

Mr. Pepys practiced the art of receiving with admirable finesse, and the *Diary* contains scores of instances of his ability to entice a gift from the King's merchants, minor officials, or anyone for whom he had done a favor. He also knew where his obligations lay and who could make plain his pathway in the daily round. The person who could advance him speediest was His Royal Highness, James, Duke of York, Lord High Admiral of the Fleet, who was the top man in the navy—higher even than His Lordship, Mr. Pepys's patron and kinsman, Edward Montagu, Earl of Sandwich. As for King Charles II, he was a kind enough man in his way, and an able man, too, if one could get him to hold still long enough to listen to anything; then he could act sensibly, quickly, and with good results. The King, however, was busy with his own private affairs, women especially; and he left matters of state to statesmen, to one of the ablest of all, his brother, the Lord High Admiral.

Mr. Pepys came to know James intimately, for they had much in common: diligence, devotion to duty, and loyalty to His Majesty. The way to reach the Lord High Admiral was *via* his able Secretary, Mr. William (later Sir William) Coventry. In a few years Mr. Pepys was able to see the Duke directly, but it was prudent and workable in these earlier years, in all matters pertaining to the navy, to move *via* Coventry. Mr. Pepys learned, too, to admire Mr. Coventry's diligence, devotion to duty, and loyalty to King Charles. Here was another man who was living proof that in the mad, merry Restoration there were good and true Englishmen who acted their part well. In fact, there were just as many such men as there were of the more notorious and better advertised clowns and profligates. There was a veritable army of major and minor officials, especially minor, who kept England on her feet and looking forward. Mr. Pepys and Mr. Coventry were of this breed, and for each other they had a mutual respect and admiration that increased with the years. Mr. Pepys had such confidence in Mr. Coventry that, when he told him that he kept a journal of events, Mr. Pepys confided that he was doing the self-same thing, the only known person to whom he gave this confidence.[8] For many years Mr. Pepys saw him almost daily.

When Mr. Pepys called on June 10 on His Lordship, the Earl of Sandwich, he drew him aside to tell him of a new honor that His Majesty had conferred. He had named the Earl of Sandwich special ambassador to Portugal to escort the Princess Katherine of Braganza, queen-to-be, to England. His Lordship's assignment included an official mission to Algiers to settle business and to put the fleet in order there; and he was then to return to Lisbon with three ships to meet a fleet that was to follow him. He wished to entrust Mr. Pepys "with the seeing of all things done in his absence as to this great preparation," and he informed Pepys that he would receive orders and instructions from the Lord Chancellor and from Mr. Edward Montagu. A confidential, responsible assignment such as this one that would also bring Pepys into direct contact with important personages would have pleased any average humble man. It filled Mr. Pepys with joy, for not only were the contacts good for a rising man, but could provide ways to make a little money. As usual, dinner being near ready, Pepys stayed for a bite and was seated at Lady Montagu's table; "but after we were set," he reports, "comes in some persons of condition, and so the children and I rose and dined by ourselves, all the children and I, and were very merry and they mighty fond of me." In such high spirits was he that he did not mind being bumped from the table to make room for persons of higher position.

Two days later when His Lordship asked Mr. Pepys to arrange to buy three hundred pounds worth of cloth to give as presents to the Turks at Barbary, Mr. Pepys made his little profit. On June 13, he accompanied His Lordship on his mission, going with him from London in the barge to Deptford where the party boarded a Dutch yacht on which Pepys had a merry time drinking and singing with his friends. When his party boarded the wherry to return to London, His Lordship ordered five volleys fired in Mr. Pepys's honor, "all they had charged," he adds and thereby insinuates that perhaps more volleys would have been fired in his honor had other guns been charged. The Clerk of the Acts was happy and proud, nevertheless, for he had rated a five-gun salute. Going toward London in the boat, he took off his shoes and stockings to enjoy the simple pleasure of bathing his feet in the water.

Returning to his desk after a drinking session at the "Dog" with the Exchequer men celebrating St. Thomas Day, December 21, 1661, Mr. Pepys was outraged when Sir William Batten and Sir William Penn seemed to reprimand him for not being at his desk, saying that without their secretary, meaning him, they could not sit as a committee. Mr. Pepys reflected that he must keep himself at a little distance from them and not be too humble, or he should never be able to keep himself even with them. Being the youngest member of the navy committee, having always to insist that his being Secretary of the Acts entitled him to the status of a commissioner, and being a sensitive man, insecure in the knowledge of his humble parentage, he constantly needed to remind himself that he was at least as good a man as Penn, Batten, or Minnes—if not quite so good as Mr. Coventry or His Lordship. Pepys waged a constant fight with what the modern psychologists call an "inferiority complex"; on most occasions he won his battles.

IV *Mr. Pepys Masters His Job*

On January 9, 1662, Mr. Pepys took another step closer to the Duke of York: The navy commissioners had discussed with him the practice of striking flags, "which will now put me upon finishing my resolution of writing something upon the subject," concludes Mr. Pepys. This habit of keeping a record—of being meticulous—was a part of the hard core of Mr. Pepys's nature.

The man who can pull a written paper out of his pocket or out of his files upon demand is always a man to respect and to watch. There were other occasions when every other official in his presence would shut his mouth while Mr. Pepys spoke to the point on a given subject, for he would have taken the trouble to do research on the subject. Whatever was the ancient custom of striking flags in respect to His Majesty's ships at sea, Mr. Pepys wanted to find out. He would find out what ships of what country's navy were entitled by right of ancient tradition and prestige to have the flags of passing ships lowered in their honor. He scented a good lead, for surely the honor would be due England's ships that for centuries had sailed the oceans of the world. He would someday broaden his study and write a history of the navy itself.

Being a practical man, he was moved by considerations other than pure love of England; he would use these studies to be the knowing man among his associates. He would make them all respect him and come to him, and there came times when the only person who could save a fellow commissioner's skin from jail was the Mr. Pepys who had kept a record. A record, moreover, could be used for a little bit of judicious flattery. He could tell Charles and James Stuart how their father, or their grandfather, had done this or that. What happened was that he made himself the indispensable man—indispensable to the Lord High Admiral, James, Duke of York, and to England herself in the perilous times to come.

Realizing that he could not be thoroughly informed unless he knew what was going on at court and in Parliament, he developed a standing practice, when Parliament was sitting, of inquiring daily what it had done. There were influential people, including nobility, who were willing to talk at length with the respectful, alert young Clerk of the Acts; and men sharp enough to notice things could see that he was admired by the Duke of York and, through him, by his brother, King Charles, and by the Duke's father-in-law, Lord Chancellor Clarendon. Then, too, Mr. Pepys had connections with the Montagu clan, the Manchesters and Mandevilles, Crewes, Wrights, and Carterets, aristocrats all. It came to be that even persons who disliked or mistrusted Mr. Pepys thought that they had better let him alone lest, in treading on his toes, they dash a foot against that of someone more powerful.

[34]

There could be no doubt at all that Mr. Pepys was a rising man, for on Sunday, April 27, 1662, James, Duke of Ormonde, the Lord High Steward, sent his coach for him; and he was recognized and spoken to by the Earl of Manchester, Lord Chamberlain, whom he followed with a crowd of gallants to chapel. The Sunday that had begun so auspiciously tapered to mediocrity. After dinner, Mr. Pepys, Sir William Batten, Ned Pickering,[9] and Dr. Timothy Clarke[10] went by coach to the navy yard and then on board the *Swallow* to hear the navy chaplain preach a sorry sermon, one full of nonsense and false Latin; but the chaplain prayed for "the Right Honourable the principal officers." Mr. Pepys was pleased since, as Clerk of the Acts, he was included among them. He rewarded the chaplain by treating him to a glass of wine after service.

Promise of a signal honor came to him at Portsmouth on April 28. He and Dr. Clarke had engaged in a scholarly discussion, and the doctor was so impressed that he offered to secure his induction into the college of virtuosos, the Royal Society; to present him to Viscount Brouncker, its president; and to give Mr. Pepys some demonstrations in anatomy. An outcome of Mr. Pepys's visit to the Portsmouth Navy Yard, April 28-30, was his drawing up instructions in those matters in which reforms and improvements seemed necessary. He secured other commissioners' signatures to the memorandum and sent it promptly to Portsmouth. The document was well timed, for the Duke of York was at Portsmouth on May 10 when it was dispatched there.

When Mr. William Coventry came to the office on June 3, 1662, and presented his patent as the new Navy Commissioner, Mr. Pepys began to do the necessary paper work to make Coventry's appointment official. He started to draw up a contract, whereupon Sir William Penn forbade him, saying that that was a duty for the Comptroller to perform and ordering Mr. Turner, the Chief Clerk, to do it. Mr. Pepys stood up to Penn. He showed him the letter containing the Duke of York's orders pertaining to his job, Mr. Barlow's letter relinquishing the position of Clerk of the Acts to him, and he acquainted him with the practice of preceding commissioners as stated by Sir George Carteret, the Treasurer, who was himself at one time the Comptroller. "It was ruled for me," says Mr. Pepys. This was one quick outcome of Mr. Pepys's habit of diligence. He had learned all he could find about his job and simply knew more about it than anyone else, and he demolished Sir William Penn in the quick, heated encounter. What Comptroller Sir John Minnes would do when he learned of the argument Mr. Pepys did not know; but Penn had behaved "like a base rascal." Pepys demonstrated on many occasions that he was a man to be reckoned with, but he admitted at home that night that his mind was troubled about Sir William's "playing the rogue" with him.

Mr. Pepys had a certain slyness in taking on authority, in timidly pawing into another man's purlieu, and in cautiously establishing squatter sovereignty if the other man turned his head or was busy with something else. Prying about in his effective way on August 13, 1662, he came upon "the greatest cheat" that he had yet found: the rope-makers of Woolwich were overcharging the King three pence a yard, and he was determined to stop this pricerigging. A few days later, August 18, he learned some additional lessons in thievery from Assistant Master Deane, who demonstrated to him how mis-measuring timber resulted in cheating the King. Mr. Pepys's zeal and competence were bringing their rewards, for Mr. Coventry noticed him with admiration and told the Earl of Sandwich and others, on August 20, that Mr. Pepys was the life of the navy office.

In the meantime, the day before, Sir George Carteret had told Mr. Pepys that Sir William Batten had complained that there were some persons at the office who would do him a bad turn. Sir George had not been aroused by the complaint, and Mr. Pepys had further reassurance of his growing influence when Sir George told him that he had spoken well of him to the Lord Chancellor and that, if Mr. Pepys wished evidence of his love for him, he should ask His Lordship to ask the Lord Chancellor what he (Sir George) had said about him. This almost femininely indirect character testimonial pleased Mr. Pepys; he loved praise and would take it wherever he found it and under whatever circumstances. More than praise came to him in this summer of 1662 for he was appointed a Commissioner for Tangier, and he accepted an assignment to be a Supervisor of the Chest (the seamen's pension fund).

By summer's end, he had made himself the most useful and necessary man at the office; for on September 8, 1662, when the Duke of York announced to the assembled navy commissioners at his quarters at St. James's that he would request a weekly report from them in keeping with the old custom, the members told His Royal Highness that Mr. Pepys would be the best person to supply it. Always ready at an instant's notice, he produced on the spot his short notes and gave the Duke a full account of what had been done recently at the navy office. He spoke then not only for himself but also for the entire navy board; he quickly consolidated his advantage and proceeded to another by proposing several things for the Duke's approval, which was given. On this occasion Mr. Pepys had proved to be the kind of colleague that makes even weak associates look good. His fellow commissioners, whatever else they might have thought of him, appreciated his ability and, occasionally, his readiness to hide their shortcomings.

An occasion, simple as it seems, that must have marked a turning point for the better in Mr. Pepys's manhood as well as in his fortunes transpired on Monday morning, January 25, 1664. At Whitehall, he made the usual courtesy stop at His Lordship's the Earl of Sandwich's lodgings before going to the Duke of York's quarters for the customary Monday morning meeting about navy affairs. On this occasion, His Lordship neither came down to him nor sent for him to come into his chambers, and Mr. Pepys simply walked away in embarrassment and, on his own initiative and alone, went to the Duke's. Hereafter he came to be increasingly reliant upon his own efforts to forge ahead in prestige and in favor with the Lord High Admiral himself. Lord Sandwich's snobbish capriciousness was one of the best things that ever happened to Mr. Pepys.

V   *Mr. Pepys Consults with the King and the Duke of York*

A steadily increasing interest in state affairs is in evidence from the outset of the *Diary*. Intensified in the middle years of the *Diary*, this concern reaches a climax after its close when Mr. Pepys sought membership in Parliament and, after failing in 1669 to be returned for Aldborough in Suffolk, was elected for Castle Rising in 1673. He could hardly have failed to be interested in public affairs, for he came into almost daily working contact with the men who actually governed England: James, Duke of York, and to a less extent his brother King Charles; George Monk, Duke of Albemarle; the Earl of Clarendon; the Duke of York's secretary, Mr. William, later Sir William Coventry; and Sir George Carteret. These men ran things; they took enough time off from wenching, His Majesty excepted, to see that the public business of England did not collapse. There were others, too, at a somewhat lower level, and others still lower than they, who would have been good, reliable public servants at any time, in any land, under any government. Mr. Pepys belonged in the second or third or fourth tier of public servants, and he was a man who would do an honest day's work and who was never a clock-watcher, the kind of man who kept England whole. He came to feel, increasingly, that the public business was his business.

Evidence of Mr. Pepys's sly caution lies in the fact that, although His Lordship had asked his advice about going to sea when Mr. Pepys already had been consulted on May 29 in the matter by Mr. Coventry, Mr. Pepys told His Lordship nothing then of the consultation; he waited for a day or two, until May 31, before he went to give the advice that His Lordship had asked. He told him what Mr. Coventry had said and got a perfectly natural response; His Lordship wondered why the Duke of York, who seemed most friendly to him, had not said a word to him of his wish to have him go to sea. His Lordship told Mr. Pepys that, were it not for the fact that he was a former parliament man and hence constantly suspect and obnoxious to the current crop of cavaliers and forced to put up with slights, he would permit no man to make a move in navy affairs without his consent. His Lordship complained, moreover, about how matters were going in the navy; commanders were being named without his knowledge, let alone his approval.

Mr. Pepys surely could be counted upon to have recognized the fact that His Lordship had slipped badly in court influence, although the King as usual thought well of him. His Majesty, nevertheless, was really a broken reed to lean upon because he was never there when a man needed him. He might be found in some lady's bed, and he simply would not hold still long enough to listen to, or to do, much of anything else. Thus it was that Mr. Pepys and His Lordship came to a decision that Mr. Pepys should tell Mr. Coventry that His Lordship was most willing to receive any commands from the Duke, however slight the assignment.

Reaching Mr. Coventry's office with the message in no time at all that same day, Mr. Pepys got a response of thinly veiled disappointment. Did His Lordship know that the Duke really did not expect him to accept such a modest command? Caught in the middle, Mr. Pepys answered affirmatively. He was in a quandary. Does the Duke think the command too small for His Lordship to accept, or is it, really, the fact that he wants to get rid of him, wants him out of the navy altogether? Suspecting the latter, Mr. Pepys concludes, "But methinks other ways might have been used to put him by, without going in this manner about it, and so I hope it is out of kindness indeed."

The fact that Mr. Pepys was now a man of considerable influence—enough to have his advice sought and heard—is in further evidence on June 4. He recounts that he spent some time with the Duke "giving him an account of how matters go, and of the necessity there is of a power to presse seamen, without which we cannot really raise men for this fleete of twelve sayle, besides that it will assert the King's power of pressing, which at present is somewhat doubted, and will make the Dutch believe we are in earnest." Granting that this type of advice would not be expected to arouse any objections, the fact remains that, for a sea-going power like England under a trifling king like Charles, it was good advice which, if followed, would strengthen the King's navy and his royal hand.

After dinner, on July 21, 1664, Mr. Pepys went to see Lord Chancellor Hyde to report to him on his management of the business of His Lordship's timber. The Lord Chancellor was pleased; and, although he carried himself with great discretion, Mr. Pepys knew that he thought his interests well served by him. When he mentioned what he had done in the Lord Chancellor's behalf to Mr. Coventry and discovered that the proceedings carried the germ of trouble, Mr. Pepys became anxious. Mr. Coventry told him on July 23 that, until the matter of timber was mentioned at the meeting of the Navy Board, he did not know that the Lord Chancellor had an interest in it; and he added that he had told the Duke of York that, if the Lord Chancellor were *his* father-in-law, he would advise him to forego a profit of two or three thousand pounds in the King's interest. Such a great man as the Lord Chancellor,[11] added Mr. Coventry, had a great many enemies who would be glad to have some advantage over him. Mr. Pepys determined to stand off from this business of timber as far as possible.

The kind of notice that he dearly loved came to him on November 9, 1664, at Whitehall where he had gone to see Sir

George Carteret. A meeting of the King's Council was in session, and Mr. Pepys was called in. In fact, he was the type who, knowing that the big folks were meeting behind closed doors, would innocently stick his head through the door and pull it back again with profuse apology. There is no record that he did this today, but he was called in "and demanded by the King himself many questions. . . ." Among those present at the Council were the Lord Chancellor, the Archbishop of Canterbury, and the Lord Treasurer;[12] and Mr. Pepys was proud that His Majesty had asked him so many questions and called his name so often in such aristocratic company.

Mr. Pepys achieved another niche in the history of men and affairs on February 15, 1665, when he was formally inducted into the Royal Society. Even if Mr. Povy,[13] who had proposed his name, was a very fool with figures, he was a man of good taste for food and wine; and he had the good sense and the good grace by this gesture to flatter Mr. Pepys and to thank him for the many maddening hours that he had spent trying to unsnarl his accounts. Mr. Pepys was unanimously approved by the experimental scientists present, including President Lord Brouncker, Sirs Philip Neale, Robert Moray, Thomas Harvey, and Drs. Boyle, Hooke, Goddard, Clarke, and Whistler. Mr. Pepys had a great time with the group at the "Crown" tavern, for he loved good talk, too; moreover, he had the wit and understanding to be at ease among scientists and philosophers.

VI *Mr. Pepys Becomes More Active in State Affairs*

It must be admitted that, in a situation that most men abhor when another than themselves is in it, Mr. Pepys was impressively effective. The situation is that of a confidential informer, who relates to a superior how things are actually going in an office, who does what, whom to trust, and the like. Although, admittedly, the Clerk of the Acts was a superior factotum at the navy office, he made himself appear even better on March 15 in a private conference with the Duke of York's personal secretary, the redoubtable Mr. William Coventry. Spending an hour with him in private discourse, Mr. Pepys says that he delivered to him many notes of things about which he would get the Duke's command. The reward for this inside information may be seen in the following observation: "He did largely owne his dependence as to the office upon my care, and received very great expressions of love from him, and so parted with great satisfaction to myself."

A surprise in the *Diary*, as well as a delight, is its emphasis upon state affairs and, specifically, the fitting out and provisioning of ships for the sea. No man, with the possible exception of the Duke of York, played a more significant role than did Mr. Pepys in readying the King's navy. Any great administrator must of necessity rely upon an anonymous person who does most of the work while the administrator does the talking and gets the credit. To indulge an innocent oversimplification, Mr. Pepys was Mr. Anonymous to the Duke of York and, indeed, to the landside of the whole British navy. It is understandable, therefore, that with the Duke returning to sea, Mr. Pepys was delighted to learn, on March 17, 1665, that, during the Duke's absence, navy matters, landside, were to be entrusted to a single command instead of to a whole parcel of chattering milords. The single command would be General George Monk, Duke of Albemarle. It did not seem odd in 1665 that an army man would be named to a post that would be the equivalent of Secretary of the Navy in the cabinet of a President of the United States. It was not an odd appointment, in any event, for the position was administrative, not nautical; and the Duke of Albemarle had proved to be a man who could get things done. He had managed the tricky job of making it possible for King Charles to land on English soil to reclaim his throne, and whole volumes could be written on the contriving, as well as on the bold venturing, that had made this restoration possible. Mr. Pepys always recognized a good man when he saw one. General Monk, Duke of Albemarle, was a painstaking, plodding man—a little on the dull side, but a good man for the King's business.

At a fine meeting of the Tangier Committee on March 20, 1665, and despite powerful rivalry for the job, Mr. Pepys was fully confirmed Treasurer for Tangier, and the Duke of York sent a paper not only recommending confirmation but also praising the worthy Clerk of the Acts. Everyone present scrambled on the bandwagon: Mr. Creed,[14] Lord Fitzharding, and others. There were such nodding of heads and smiling and audible whispering of how fine a man Mr. Pepys was that he made the understandable human error of reporting "all full of joy" at his appointment. He had taken a considerable step up in the world.

Praise was music to Mr. Pepys's ears; and, when it came from another good public servant or from his aristocratic superiors, it was especially valuable. On March 22, he reports visiting Mr. Coventry, who tendered something more valuable than praise.[15] It was a friendship of the heart, love and esteem in generous measure; and Mr. Pepys was gratified, stating that he would place a higher value on no man's friendship. Later in the day, at St. James's, he received the Duke of York's compliments and expressions of his value to him; and Mr. Pepys expressed yet another superlative: "which comforted me above all things in the world." In the crowd come to bid the Duke goodbye upon his going to sea, Mr. Pepys saw Edmund Waller, the poet; and he thought enough of this chance encounter to say that he had never seen Mr. Waller before. It is understandable that Mr. Pepys should be so casual as to write, "by coach home with W. Pen who was there," omitting the "Sir" that he always used in writing of him.

The first meeting with the Duke of Albemarle, since his taking charge of the Navy Board in the Duke of York's stead, was held on March 27. Quite humanly, Mr. Pepys took the Duke's measure, but his estimate of him, though satisfactory enough, is understandably not conclusive: His Grace was a quiet heavy man, who would help business when he could and hinder nothing. After waiting his chance to speak alone to His Grace, Mr. Pepys thanked him for approving the Tangier appointment; and the Duke received Mr. Pepys's thanks kindly and spoke of his personal esteem of him. When Mr. Pepys paid the same courtesy call and said similar respectful things to Secretary of State Sir Henry Bennet, he received similar compliments and an additional courtesy from Sir Henry of being given some official letters to read. Mr. Pepys's political sure-handedness and sure-footedness are obvious. He could beat any man by dropping behind when a meeting adjourned to say the last word to the presiding officer. Then, too, hardly a living man is impervious to a little oil lightly laid on, and Mr. Pepys knew how to "oil" a man.

At Whitehall, on April 17, 1665, King Charles saw Mr. Pepys and came to him, called him by name, and talked with him concerning the ships of the navy. "And this is the first time that ever I knew the King did know me personally; so that hereafter I must not go thither, but with expectation to be questioned, and to be ready to give good answers," says Mr. Pepys, pleased with the royal recognition and making a wise resolution.

Now that His Lordship's star had begun to set, this was the time for Mr. Pepys to seek elsewhere for strength and security. With a magnificent sense of political timing, he turned to his old friend Sir William Coventry, Secretary and Administrative Assistant to the Lord High Admiral of the Fleet, James, Duke of York. The office of Surveyor General of the Victualling needed filling, and Mr. Pepys knew, as did everyone else, that he knew more about provisioning the fleet than did any man in England. Would Sir William Coventry think so too? He should, for Sir William was a sound man and as straightforward a one as could be in these crooked times. Mr. Pepys wrote to him on October 19 to ask point-blank to be appointed to the position.

Appointed to the important post of Surveyor General of the Victualling on October 27, Mr. Pepys was deeply gratified not only with the post itself but also with the expressions of confidence in his worthiness by the dukes of York and Albemarle and by Sir William Coventry. For this long step upward, Mr. Pepys gave God much of the credit, but he kept much for himself. He thanked God, adding "to see that as I do take pains, so God blesses me, and hath sent me masters that do observe that I take pains," a truth simply but eloquently expressed.

When he learned that the King, the Duke of York, and the Court would be at Hampton Court on Sunday, January 28, 1666, Mr. Pepys decided to make an effective appearance there. Wisely, he decided not to overdress; he wore his almost-new velvet coat and a plain cravat, took a hackney coach to Lord Brouncker's, joined Milord in his coach-and-four, and headed for Hampton Court. Mr. Pepys loved praise as much, almost, as he loved money; and he got a generous amount of it from His Majesty, the Duke of York, and Sir William Coventry. The King said, "Mr. Pepys, I do give you thanks for your good service all this year, and I assure you I am very sensible of it." The Duke praised his manual of instructions to the pursers, and Sir William Coventry assured him of his respect and love and his concern for his health in this time of sickness. That night, lying abed at an inn in Kingston, Mr. Pepys reported that he slept soundly, his mind being in a great delirium between joy for what the King, the Duke, and Sir William Coventry had said to him and trouble for Lord Sandwich's concernments. But Mr. Pepys would manage to preserve himself from indefinite sadness for his inept Lordship.

Trying his wings, as it were, in order to discover if his newly discovered confidence would support him at Court, Mr. Pepys, on Sunday, February 11, 1666, reported that he contrived a garment to be in mourning at Court for the King of Spain. Whatever grief he may have felt for the departed monarch, Mr. Pepys had other ideas in mind. He wanted to see if, perchance, no unfavorable notice would be taken of him as he strutted about, trotted behind, or dogged the footsteps of bona-fide courtiers: "I to the Parke, and walked two or three turnes of the Pell Mell with the company about the King and Duke; the Duke speaking to me a good deal. . . ." He achieved his goal in a sense, for none turned him away and all had a kind word to say to him.

Mr. Pepys had a fine trait, a minor one, that helped his political climb. He was a good listener, and important people want to be listened to. After a short meeting with the Duke of York on April 21, 1666, Mr. Pepys and Lord Brouncker were strolling in Whitehall Garden, when King Charles met them and told them a joke or two, using tolerable puns, at the expense of Sir William Batten, Commissioner Christopher Pett, and Captain Taylor. Mr. Pepys rewarded His Majesty for all time by recording the jokes in the *Diary*.

Walking with Captain Erwin through the Park at Greenwich on June 2, Mr. Pepys could plainly hear the guns at sea. England was in a seeming interminable naval war with the Dutch. Pepys and the Captain went to the "King's Head" and ordered steaks for four o'clock. While the meal was cooking, reports Mr. Pepys, they walked to the waterside; then, seeing the King and Duke come down in their barge to Greenwich-house, they joined them; and Mr. Pepys spoke to the King of his activities. The royal brothers could not have appeared at a time more propitious to Mr. Pepys's opportunity to tell them that he, really, was managing the war, landside. His Majesty should have knighted Mr. Pepys on the spot.

The shortage of money for the conduct of the navy office had become so severe that the Clerk of the Acts decided to take direct action by setting forth the problem in writing for the consideration of King Charles and the Duke of York. He shut himself in his room at home on the afternoon of November 17, 1666, to finish his "great letter" exposing the ill condition of the navy so known to him that it would be impossible for the King not to understand the dire circumstances. Mr. Pepys, furthermore, appeared sanguine that his letter would cause money to be found and all matters set right, or else peace with the Dutch would be sought on any terms. On the following morning, Sunday, November 18, he got up by candlelight and walked to Whitehall where he met by appointment Lord Brouncker and Sir William Coventry, read his letter to them, and got from them what the busy seeker generally gets under similar circumstances, human nature being what it is: their approval of the letter. Pepys had good sense enough to realize, nevertheless, that a critical letter of this type had inherent dangers; but he had written it literally for love of England and in an effort to save her. His customary self-seeking aside, this act was that of a courageous conscientious public servant, and this day's entry in the *Diary* justifies it: "and as I do our business in defence of the Board, so I think it is as good a letter in the manner, and I believe it is the worst in the matter of it, as ever came from any office to a Prince."

The reaction of Commissioners Batten and Penn to Mr. Pepys's letter was understandable: they resented it. Mr. Pepys, who had the gift of fooling himself, said that, although Sir William Batten signed the letter, he would not go with him to Whitehall to deliver it to King and Council; however, he had liked the letter. Sir William Penn simply had not waited to sign the letter that was being copied by Mr. Hewer.[16] Mr. Pepys took it on to Whitehall, met Lord Brouncker, who signed it, delivered it to Mr. Chiffinch,[17] who took it in to Sir William Coventry who presented it to "the King and Council being sitting"; there, says Mr. Pepys, "I leave it to its fortune."

Among the reactions to the letter that he got next day was Sir George Carteret's. He was quite displeased that Mr. Pepys had sent it to the King and Council without consulting him, but Pepys was confident enough that the truth and sheer merit of his letter would justify it and him in the presence of anybody's ill will. He was really on the threshold of the place where he could risk making an enemy to gain an ally—if the ally were powerful enough. And in this case he would be, for he would be the Lord High Admiral of the Fleet, himself, James, Duke of York. Mixing pleasure with business, Mr. Pepys stopped off at the "Bull-head" tavern, had six bottles of claret filled, and sent them as a gift to Mrs. Martin.[18]

After a visit to Brampton and on his first full day in town (Sunday, October 13, 1667), Mr. Pepys, quite understandably, sought out the influential ones: James, Duke of York, and others. At St. James's, he found His Royal Highness dressing, and many lords and members of Parliament going in and out of his room to kiss his hand. The Duke of York singled Mr. Pepys out to tell him that he had spoken to the King, and that His Majesty had given Mr. Pepys the little ship, *The Maybolt*, that he had asked for. His Royal Highness assured Mr. Pepys, moreover, that he was mighty satisfied with his service and that he would be willing to do anything in his power for him. Mr. Pepys thanked him "and departed with mighty joy." He seemed to sense that he had made still another beginning with the Duke of York, moving closer to him in confidence and respect.

When he told Sir William Penn that afternoon that he had been given the little ship, Sir William offered to send for the captain of *The Maybolt* and to command him to furnish it as for a long voyage at His Majesty's expense. Mr. Pepys's reaction to the suggestion was to seem to ignore it, to note how much more valuable Sir William's proposal would make *The Maybolt*, and to conclude that Sir William was a knave to the King for having made the suggestion, just as he had been one to Mr. Pepys on occasion. He, nevertheless, accepted Sir William's offer.

VII *Mr. Pepys Impresses Parliament*

From October 20-21, 1667, the Clerk of the Acts learned from many sources that the Parliament in session was most zealous in inquiring into just about anything that had gone awry in England during the recent months, and especially into whatever pertained to the bad conduct of the naval war with the Dutch. He knew that as Clerk of the Acts, as the most articulate Commissioner, and as one recognized by his colleagues as their spokesman, he would be called upon someday to defend the navy office. Always susceptible to flattery, he was glad to hear from this or that person that the people thought well of him and that he had built a reputation for being a dutiful man. On October 21, Mr. Pepys waited anxiously outside the Parliament house to be summoned by an investigating committee and told what answers the Navy Commissioners would be commanded to give concerning the recent Dutch War, but not until seven o'clock at night was he called in and ordered to bring all of his fellow officers to attend a parliamentary hearing the next afternoon. And Cousin Roger Pepys, M.P., whispered to him that the Parliament had decided to blame a recent naval fiasco at Chatham, on the Commissioners of the Navy. It seemed that Parliament was willy-nilly assigning blame and demanding defenses: "to lay the fault heavy somewhere and to punish it."

Cousin Roger cautioned him, moreover, what the Parliament would ask and advised him what questions might unexpectedly be put to him. His head swam with thoughts of the hearing next day; but, instead of collapsing in anxious panic, he armed himself with facts and figures and with piles of impressive looking papers. Getting out of bed about four o'clock on the morning of October 22, he went to his office, put his papers and his ideas in sequential order, and worked all morning and through the dinner hour, driving his clerks to hand him this and that paper until he was ready by early afternoon. He and Commissioners Penn, Harvey, and Brouncker went by coach to the hearing; but Sir William Penn, who promptly took the sanctuary of his seat as a member of Parliament, left the other three to do the defending.

When they were called in, Mr. Pepys was singled out for deference; he had so much paper paraphernalia that a chair had to be brought to rest it in. Commissioner Pett, resident at Chatham during the war, was there as a defendant and made a fool of himself by plunging in to answer questions even before they were propounded, or by answering what he should have left for others to answer. Waiting until he was asked something, Mr. Pepys, contrariwise, consulted his papers and read interminable answers, talking his way through or around this or that tricky problem, until candles had to be brought to light his way through still other books and papers. The Parliament was impressed into speechless admiration, and adjourned. "And my Cozen Pepys did come out and joy me," modestly admits Mr. Pepys, so well had he acquitted himself. Many persons praised his performance, and his fellow officers were so proud of themselves for Mr. Pepys's masterful defense of the navy office that they were "all very brisk to see themselves so well acquitted."

Goodnaturedly, Mr. Pepys admitted that their briskness made him a little proud. He lightheartedly went home in Sir William Penn's coach, ate a good supper, and went to bed with an easy mind.

As might be expected after such an impressive appearance before the Parliament, Mr. Pepys was in high spirits on the following day, October 24. Although Sir William Coventry was being harassed by the Parliament, he was kind enough to tell Mr. Pepys that the House had been well pleased with his report. Himself a little cocky, Mr. Pepys reports that he walked a few turns with Commissioner Pett, and "did give the poor weak man" some advice about how to better his pleading for himself. He paid a visit to Mrs. Martin, was entertained fully, and was in such generous spirits that he left three pounds with her to buy his god-daughter her first new gown.

Hearing of a genuine compliment paid him, if indirectly, the previous day, when he was absent from a meeting of the Tangier Committee, the Clerk of the Acts went to Whitehall, on January 15, 1669, where he met King Charles and the Duke of York. At the previous day's meeting when someone had proposed a new system of paying the garrison, the Duke would not permit discussion of the matter to continue unless Mr. Pepys were present. When he thanked His Royal Highness for this recognition, James answered that one who minded the King's business as diligently as Mr. Pepys deserved respect. Thus had developed across the crowded years of the *Diary* the intimate confidence between the Duke of York and Mr. Pepys that led to his appointment, in 1672, to the high position of Secretary of the Admiralty.

It has often been shown that Mr. Pepys was the type of man who would ask to be appointed to a vacancy even before there was one for him to fill. He proposed to Sir William Coventry, on February 19, 1669, his "putting in to serve in Parliament, if there should . . . be a new one chose," and he states that Sir William liked the idea mightily for the sake of the King, navy, and the Duke of York; and Sir William promised to propound the idea to the Duke. It would be difficult under the circumstances to deny modest-seeming Mr. Pepys a rotten-borough seat in Parliament—especially since he would serve his patrons, not himself.

CHAPTER 3

Typical Days with Mr. Pepys

ONE of the chief activities of Mr. Pepys's average day was making money, and it would be only a mild exaggeration to state that Mr. Pepys kept his palm outstretched. He got rich from gifts, graft, service charges, and interest rates. He became a genius in scenting a profit and in hinting to suppliers that it would speed matters if they showed proper respect to the Clerk of the Acts, Victualler, and Secretary of the King's Navy, Samuel Pepys. Beginning almost from his first day as a navy official, he accepted gifts in cash or in kind. The Earl of Sandwich, on his part, believed too literally in the advice to collect emoluments that he had given Mr. Pepys; and the fact of the matter is that the Earl lacked Mr. Pepys's skill and circumspection: for, while Mr. Pepys prospered, the Earl got into difficulty and was moved into the shadows.

The most profitable sources of gifts in kind were the sea captains and other sea-going persons. And marvelous gifts they were. Captain Burr sent Pepys four dozen bottles of wine on August 24, 1660. Three days later, Mr. Pierce, the purser, sent him a vessel of Northdown ale; Captain Cuttance sent a fine Turkish rug and a jar of olives; and John Burr sent a pair of fine turtledoves to Mrs. Pepys. In a way of speaking, through the long years ahead, the wealth of the Indies, the spiced dainties from silken Samarkand and cedared Lebanon, manna and dates in argosy transferred from Fez, rich prizes from ships guided into English ports by rude sailors in whose veins still coursed the pirates' blood of Drake, Raleigh, and Frobisher, found their way into the cupboards and strong boxes of Mr. Samuel Pepys, Esq.

He did not need a whole year to be convinced of the truth of His Lordship's observation that the wages accruing to a job were a minor part of its emoluments. He had received miscellaneous sums throughout 1660; and gifts of food, wine, and a trinket now and then were frequent. He graduated to big-time bounty toward the end of the year. In fact, there were many who wanted favors done at the office: a contract for victualling the navy, or to supply cordage for the ships, or raw hemp and tar, or sailcloth, or cloth for flags. The paper work for all these transactions was Mr. Pepys's responsibility as Clerk of the Acts, and he did nothing unethical for his day when he accepted a gift in money or in goods or when he peddled his influence to the highest or the most persistent bidder. One of the chief of his benefactors was smooth-working Mr. Dennis Gauden, who, on December 19, 1660, gave him "a great chine of beef and half a dozen tongues" for the on-coming Christmastide.

I *Benefactors*

On July 21, 1664, Mr. Gauden, Navy Victualler, gave Mr. Pepys his proudest household possession: a massive pair of silver flagons in fine leather cases, so noble a gift that Mr. Pepys had misgivings as to whether or not to keep it. This splendid gift sent him into such high spirits that he went to Betty Lane's lodgings in Westminster "to give her joy." On December 8, 1665, Mr. Gauden presented the sum of five hundred pounds for paying him four thousand pounds, a half of his balance for the Tangier victualling when, indeed, Mr. Pepys had expected only one hundred pounds. Another five hundred was paid Pepys on February 4, 1667, for paying Gauden the balance on the victualling account; and there were other substantial gifts, too. Against all rivals, Mr. Pepys supported this loyal affluent influential friend.

Sir William Warren, although he did not give such prodigious single bounties as did Gauden, operated even more smoothly and, in aggregate, gave Mr. Pepys just as much. He mentioned Warren first on December 29, 1660, as coming to see him about ship timber for His Lordship. A busy timber merchant and shipbuilder to His Majesty, Warren wished, of course, to secure as many contracts as possible from the navy office, including contracts to supply timber to other shipbuilders. An instance of Mr. Pepys's profitable dealing with Warren occurred on June 23, 1662, when he came to the navy office to see Mr. Pepys. When the business was completed, the conversation turned to fir and pine boards; and the crafty Mr. Pepys offered "to go along with him among his deal ships." He learned much on this tour during which they inspected six ships: the difference between types of lumber, their cutting, trimming, and transportation and the reason why boards were increasing in price. Mr. Warren showed Mr. Pepys his vast lumberyards and took him into his fine house for a friendly glass of mum. In subsequent contacts with Sir William Warren about matters pertaining to timber, rope, tar, and other material, Mr. Pepys became a master of discovering the sleights, tricks, and schemes whereby almost every man was stuffing his pockets with His Majesty's pounds, shillings, and pence.

II *Profitable Contacts*

During a spell of sickness when Mr. Pepys had been confined to his lodgings, Sir William Warren stopped by on February 10, 1663, to pay his respects and to leave a letter and a box at the door. Mr. Pepys noted that Warren's letter mentioned giving him and Mrs. Pepys a pair of white gloves but, opening the box, they found other gifts: a fair state dish of silver and a cup that had his arms already cut upon them; they were worth, he estimated, about eighteen pounds. If Sir William had been a poet, some symbolic meaning might have been read into the gift of white gloves. As it turned out, the little matter of sending gloves for Mr. Pepys instead of Mrs. Pepys gave Sir William a chance to redeem the oversight in a very charming gesture. Almost a year later, much profitable business having passed between them, he and Mr. Pepys repaired on February 2, 1664, to the "Sun" after a long office discourse on the topic of how advantageous a war with the Dutch would be for English trade. Sir William gave him a pair of gloves wrapped in paper for Mrs. Pepys; and, feeling something hard in the package, Mr. Pepys almost died in curious anticipation of what it might be. He was hard put to get his wife to leave the room to discover the contents of the package, but he reported: "she being gone, it proves a payre of white gloves for her and forty pieces in good gold, which did so cheer my heart, that I could eat no victuals almost for dinner for joy to think how God do bless us every day more and more, and more yet he will upon the increase of my duty and endeavours. I was at a great loss what to do, whether [to] tell my wife of it or no . . . for fear of making her think me to be in a better condition . . . than yet I am."

III *Reciprocal Courtesies*

Many contracts came Sir William's way, directed to him fairly
and squarely, by Mr. Pepys: one for almost a thousand Gottenburg masts on July 21, 1664, "the biggest [contract] that ever
was made in the Navy," was Mr. Pepys's comment, "wholly of my
compassing and a good one I hope it is, for the King." Sir William
often needed Mr. Pepys's prompting to pay for favors done, and
he could hedge on occasion. On August 2, 1664, he told Mr.
Pepys that he was aware that everyone had to earn a living and
that he was willing that Mr. Pepys share with him in anything
that he dealt in. This offer was a good business one, but the
Clerk of the Acts was always chary of business involvements
that required his own money; moreover, he was no merchant.
What was more to his liking was Sir William's admission of
being obligated to him for one hundred pounds for his service
and friendship in effecting the "great contract," and his promise
to transmit a hundred pounds to him between this time and
Christmas. Sir William sent him a most handsome gift two days
later in lieu of hard cash: a splendid mare which he rode proudly
to Cousin Will Joyce's.[1]

Hope long deferred might have been the cause of Mr. Pepys's
sharpness in negotiating still another contract with Sir William
for New England masts on August 12, 1664. He made Sir William
angry, but Pepys thought it fit to do so in the King's and his
own behalf. His impatience took a sharper turn when, on September 14, he asked Sir William to lend him one hundred pounds.
By this rather coarse reminder, Sir William was made to admit
his obligation to Mr. Pepys who confided to the *Diary* that he
hoped by this means to get his hundred pounds in two or three
days. Sir William slipped the money to him two days later in a
bag at the "Sun." When Mr. Pepys offered his note, Sir William
declined, saying that the little bag was tendered purely as a
courtesy and in strict confidence between them.

By October 13, 1665, however, Mr. Pepys's disenchantment
with Sir William had begun, for he admitted being displeased
with him about a small business matter. When Lord Brouncker
provided a great dinner on board the East India ship on October 23, among the invited guests were Mr. Pepys and Sir William Warren; but Mr. Pepys had no reason to believe that the

new Navy Commissioner might be a rival for Sir William's favors and confidence. On November 2, Sir William gave Mr. Pepys a hundred pounds and promised him over a hundred more for settling a deal concerning Tangier boats. On January 26, 1666, Sir William settled handsomely with Mr. Pepys to the extent of three hundred and twenty pounds; and, as usual, this bounteous windfall prompted Mr. Pepys to "bless God."

Other business transactions profitable to Pepys were concluded from time to time, and hope of still another hundred pounds came to him on August 11 when he visited Mr. John Colvill, the goldsmith, and came to an agreement with him concerning a twenty-six hundred pound assignment on the Exchequer to Sir William Warren; but Pepys discovered on the 13th to his great joy that he would receive, instead, two hundred and thirty pounds upon bringing the transaction, involving the twenty-six hundred pounds, to a close. "God be praised for it!" breathes Mr. Pepys in a great sigh of relief.

He probably missed the real point of a conversation with Sir William at the navy office on January 11, 1667. Sir William told him that he had come to an understanding with Lord Brouncker who had promised him most particular inward friendship but not to appear at the Navy Board to have done so; and Sir William averted any suspicions of shifting loyalties by cautioning Mr. Pepys that Lord Brouncker, who had taken special notice of the fine silver flagons that he had seen at Mr. Pepys's house at a recent dinner, had merrily but enviously said that Mr. Pepys could not have got them honestly. Mr. Pepys resolved to be on guard against this ignoble soul, but also to show him that he was no mean fellow but one who could have what he pleased. Of Warren, Mr. Pepys expressed only the highest opinion on this occasion.

By January 26, 1667, Mr. Pepys had become alert to Sir William's double-dealing. He was irritated in observing how Warren was courting Lord Brouncker's favor, and he stated that Brouncker neither would nor could do any man much favor at the Navy Board, especially over Mr. Pepys himself. His thoughts made him angry, especially the idea that Sir William would value any man's friendship above his. This jealous, angry outburst was induced by Mr. Pepys's realization that Navy Commissioner Lord Brouncker was elbowing him aside from the trough filled by Sir William from which Mr. Pepys had for so long been feeding so well. Relationships between him and his partner-benefactor deteriorated rapidly, and they differed and quarreled frequently. Mr. Pepys condemned Sir William's accounts and at board meetings seemed his very enemy.

On May 24, nevertheless, Mr. Pepys admits craftily that his posture toward Warren was such that, upon good conditions from him, he would return to be his friend. This carefully conceived plan of retrieving Sir William's loyalty and largesse appeared to be working effectively, and he put it to the test when he met him on the Exchange on November 1 and fell in pace with him while going toward the "Sun" tavern. He asked Sir William's advice in disposing of a little galliot given him by the Duke of York, and Sir William agreed to think about it and to act to Mr. Pepys's best advantage. The Clerk of the Acts led the conversation into a discussion of Sir William's service and promised assistance with contrived indifference.

On December 11, 1667, Sir William actually went to Mr. Pepys's lodgings to discuss business of mutual interest. They had, by this time, renewed business discussions; and Warren was again giving his customary good advice. On this occasion he told Mr. Pepys that Parliament in its present mood would rout the King's partisans from their jobs, but that he thought Mr. Pepys would be safe enough. Sir William could also drop a sly hint. Another meeting followed on December 13, but since these were currently bad times for business, the conversation dealt with nothing substantial in the way of money.

IV *Parliament Investigates*

The fractious Parliament then in session was looking into public matters with partisan zeal, and transactions involving large sums of money soon drew parliamentary attention. The Committee on Accounts wanted to look at the books of the Navy Board, and the snarled Warren accounts were to be scrutinized. Sir William's anxiety was, therefore, understandable; and he was angry with the Board. In a conversation on February 17, 1668, at the "Ordinary" near Temple Bar, he reminded Mr. Pepys of his recent coldness toward him; and Sir William spoke also in defiance of the Navy Board. Mr. Pepys quite naturally was alert to the possible danger of Sir William's disclosing their transactions to the parliamentary Committee of Accounts. He adds that, even though Sir William were still a cunning fellow, he would find it necessary to be fair to him and to hold his tongue. The Parliament, in the meantime, continued to probe here and there, hoping to lay bare the shocking cases of graft that all were privy to. Sir William, on February 25, 1668, told Mr. Pepys that the House wanted to know what presents he and others had given to the members of the Navy Board; but he reassured him that he had denied all even though he was forsworn as to what related to Mr. Pepys.

Although this news was alarming, Mr. Pepys utterly vindicated the Navy Board and himself in his great speech before the Parliament on March 5, 1668, for which he had fortified himself with half a pint of mulled sack and a shot of brandy. The testy business of Sir William's accounts was not quite settled by Mr. Pepys's oratory, for on June 1, 1668, Warren complained to him that the Commissioners of Parliament were pressing him for explanations. Mr. Pepys was concerned that for himself some inconveniences and troubles might be occasioned, but he found temporary release from worry by visiting Mrs. Martin at Westminster.

Sir William Warren's difficulties with the Commissioners of Parliament who were looking into his accounts, although thorny, were not disastrous. On August 11, Mr. Pepys stated that he visited Sir William Coventry at Whitehall and found him troubled at the Commissioners of Accounts who continued in their determination to pry into the Warren accounts, but zealous legislative bodies are famous the world over for wishing to adjourn in August. Perhaps Mr. Pepys sensed that this Parliament was no exception, for he said that prying into Sir William's accounts was a ridiculous thing and could come to nothing but contempt. The Parliament met on August 11, long enough to adjourn until November 10.

Mr. Pepys spent all the morning of October 19 on Sir William's business, not saying what the nature of his efforts were; but he was no doubt trying to square his accounts and put them in presentable shape against any eventuality. Sir William pleaded with Mr. Pepys on Sunday, November 29, 1668, to do something to help him rectify his Gottenburg accounts which Mr. Pepys knew would never be approved unless he himself worked on them; but he confessed his unwillingness to touch them on three counts: because of fear, unwillingness to wrong the King, and the lack of profit to himself. He expressed, however, condescending pity for Warren, who for so long had suffered such great inconvenience "from the negligence of this Board."

V *Profitable Finesse*

One of Sir William Warren's annoying habits was the signifying threat. In the conversation he told Mr. Pepys that, when he saw his new coach this morning, "he wished that the owner might not contract envy by it." For this sly dig, Pepys answered Warren that it was to his advantage to keep a coach and that it would be a shame if, after eight years of hard work, he should not be thought able to afford one. Whatever dealings he and Sir William Warren would have in the future, the trusting, easy, friendly, and mutually profitable association was at an end.

To get money by one means or another was the constant concern of Pepys; and, when Captain Grove talked to him at the office on March 25, 1663, about hiring some ships to go to Tangier, Mr. Pepys hinted that he desired to make some lawful profit in the transaction. The Captain made a generous, inclusive promise to tell all that he got and to give him a share. Cautious as ever, Mr. Pepys comments that he did not demand but silently consented to the deal, but he perceived that something would be got thereby. It did not take Captain Grove long to respond favorably to Mr. Pepys's hint of March 25 that he would like to make a little something from the Tangier transaction. On April 3, at Whitehall, he handed him a letter; and Mr. Pepys, feeling something hard inside, decided modestly not to open it in the Captain's presence but to wait until he reached the office. Breaking open the envelope and shaking all the money out of it, he looked inside the empty paper, stating that he did this in order to be able to say, if ever he should be questioned, that he saw no money in it. There were a gold piece and four pounds in silver in the envelope. Even for Mr. Pepys, who could find a way to excuse anything that he did, this self-defense was, indeed, brittle.

One Mr. Abrahall who wished to share in the supply of chandlery to His Majesty's ships sent Mrs. Pepys a fine Japanese gown on December 12, 1663. It pleased her well and came at a very opportune time to supplement her wardrobe, but Mr. Pepys did not quite know how to conduct himself since he had already accepted a gift from Mrs. Russell, also interested in the chandlery. He was now in the pay of both. On the same day, he cleared some papers with Sir George Carteret in Captain Taylor's behalf, for which small service he hoped to gain five pounds. Then, at his invitation, Mr. Luellin joined him at dinner and told him that Mr. Dering was offering him fifty pounds if he would take some goods off his hands and, further, that, if Mr. Pepys would support Dering in securing his patent as the King's merchant, he could spare him two hundred pounds a year from his profits. The sum of two hundred pounds would be a good salary in itself for any modest man in almost any century.

The manner in which Mr. Pepys lulled his conscience into a profitable decision can best be told by himself: "I was glad to hear both of these, but answered him no further than that as I would not by anything be bribed to be unjust in my dealings, so I was not so squeamish as not to take people's acknowledgement where I had the good fortune by my pains to do them good and just offices, and so I would not come to be at any agreement with him, but I would labour to do him this service and to expect his consideration thereof afterwards as he thought fit." This statement is, in fact, a manifesto of Mr. Pepys's attitude toward gratuities, handouts, and service-charges; for, although he rarely turned any man away, he would not, on the other hand, accept an outright bribe. He was also cautious enough to leave an avenue of escape for the future so that, if any accusations were brought of bribery or sharp dealing, he could always claim that he had merely accepted a gift as a token of appreciation. What was wrong with this formula was that it could not be made to fit all cases.

Many people came to confer with the rising, thriving young official on New Year's Day, 1664. One brought "the best New Year's gift that ever I had," says Mr. Pepys, a bill of exchange from Mr. Dering drawn upon himself for payment of fifty pounds to Mr. Luellin. This stratagem would protect Mr. Pepys's fine business hand. That palpitating conscience of his still bothered him a little; he would not take all of the gift, "or if I do then give some of it to Luellin," he shakily resolved, perhaps seeking the prop of a partner in guilt. One almost wishes that Pepys had taken these gifts and not been so finicky about them; but, then, where would be all the fun in the *Diary* had he not been so "persnickety"?

Mr. Falconer, Clerk of the Rope Yard at Woolwich, who came to visit on February 11, 1664, brought a fine present for Mrs. Pepys: a silver state cup and cover, worth three or four pounds; on the spot, Mr. Pepys pinned a mental price tag on any gift. Mr. Falconer's present was a little token in appreciation "for the courtesy I did him the other day," but Mr. Pepys ruminates: "I am almost sorry for this present, because I would have reserved him for a place to go in summer avisiting at Woolwich with my wife." What a thought! He is saying that it is too bad that Mr. Falconer had headed him off with a gift, for he had planned to move in on him for a nice, free summer vacation and to take Mrs. Pepys along. Next day, February 12, he took Mr. Falconer's gift to the goldsmith's, had it appraised, and found it worth £5:16. He also appraised a little cup that Joyce Norton, his cousin, had given them, value 17/-. Total value was £6:13/-, and he turned the two gifts in on a fine tankard that cost £6:10/-, and pocketed the change of 3/-.

VI *Profits and Prestige Increase*

Studying always "how to get something" for himself, Mr. Pepys was overjoyed to learn on July 16, 1664, that the contract for the Tangier victualling was to bring to him, personally, three hundred pounds a year. That sum alone would have been a good salary for a good man; although he might not have fully sensed the fact, he was really on his way to undreamed of wealth in the near future. He was shrewd enough, moreover, to secure, on July 16, Mr. Moore's signature for a payment from Sir George Carteret of one hundred and nine pounds toward reducing His Lordship's personal debt to him, thus reducing the amount to less than five hundred pounds.

A sign of Mr. Pepys's steady rise in the world may be seen in the circumstance of the meeting, on December 7, 1664, on Tangier business at his house. Lord Rutherford, wealthy Alderman Backewell, and Messrs. Povy and Creed remained for dinner. Expressing regret for having no better cheer for Mr. Povy, Mr. Pepys observed in his diary that "the foole" could be useful and that he was a cunning fellow in his way—a strange way that he had found in no other man, or could describe. Mr. Pepys was seldom so lost for words or for perceptiveness. What he saw in Mr. Povy was a man of parts and of devious resilience; he saw

Mr. Pepys in Mr. Povy. Men are quick to recognize, and some-times to admire, themselves in other men.

On December 9, he stopped at Mr. Povy's office, and there, after answering a few troublesome questions, he received a note for £117:5/- as payment for his efforts to secure bottom on the *William* for Mr. Povy's merchandise to Tangier, but his joy was tempered by Mr. Povy's metallic way in a business deal. Mr. Pepys feared that he might one day have to give an accounting for this bounty. After he had taken the note to Alderman Viner and received the money, he took it home to find Captain Taylor of the *Union* waiting with a promise of fifty pounds for still an-other Tangier deal. "For all which the Lord be praised," he added.

Gifts and gratuities steadily increased as Mr. Pepys's station improved. He would take a step upward on a day, upward in rank or in the confidence and respect of his superiors—and on that day or the next a tangible token of his rising influence would come. The day after a significant conference with the Duke of York's powerful secretary, William Coventry, on March 15, 1665, Mr. Harris, who held a contract to supply sails to the navy, sent Mr. Pepys a noble pair of silver candlesticks and snuffers and a stand to set them on; and Mr. Andrews gave him thirty-six pounds for benefits received in the Tangier contract. Mr. Pepys went to bed weary but expressed his thanks to God for these benefits. And in four days came Mr. John Burrowes, Navy Slopseller, with two large state cups, costing about six pounds each, to add to Mr. Pepys's growing collection of silver plate.

Despite the stalking pestilence, a source of great joy came to Mr. Pepys on August 23, 1665. Mr. Andrews, victualling con-tractor for Tangier, settled some outstanding Tangier accounts from which Mr. Pepys received a commission in the magnificent sum of £222:13/-. When, on August 28, Will Hewer brought home to him £119 for office disbursements, he rejoiced that he had eighteen hundred pounds and more in his house; and he thanked God that he had very little money laid out that he could not very easily recall. He then added that this was the best financial posture of his life, both as to quantity and cer-tainty, for he had most of his money in his own hand. Resolving to move temporarily to Woolwich, he was understandably wor-ried about what disposition to make of so much ready money in his Seething Lane lodgings, and he decided to risk locking it up in an iron chest. After packing several needful things and sending them forward, he joined Mrs. Pepys at Woolwich on August 28.

Returning from two days' dalliance with the ladies (December 17-18, 1665) to more tangible achievements—and let no one make the mistake of thinking that these tangible achievements were ever out of his mind—Mr. Pepys related how on December 22 he had sent for Mr. Andrews and had maneuvered the conversation so that the merchant expressed the desire to have some settlement for the victuals supplied the Tangier garrison. Mr. Pepys cleared £210 on the transaction and declared that this money was a noble addition to his "considerable" recent profits. Totaling his accounts at year's end, on December 31, he found that his money had increased from thirteen hundred to well over four thousand pounds. And he gave credit to God, to diligence, to his Tangier Treasuryship, and to the Surveyor Generalship of the Victualling for the phenomenal increase. His fortune would be doubled and redoubled in the years to come.

It has been demonstrated on numerous occasions that Mr. Pepys's favorite device for making money was insistence on a percentage from persons holding contracts for supplies to the navy. In order to pay him his fee, the contractor, naturally, charged more for his goods and services; but, by doing so, he, too, was compromised. Mr. Pepys could therefore feel quite sure that the transaction would be kept a secret. When Mr. Yeabsley, partner in a contract for supplying the Tangier garrison, was finally voted partial payment of seven thousand pounds by the Tangier Committee on July 14, 1666, Mr. Pepys was assured of a share. During the transactions, he sat fascinated as he observed Lord Ashley's[2] adroit conduct of the bill to get the money paid, for Mr. Pepys knew quite well that Lord Ashley would also get a share of it. There was, indeed, no lesson Mr. Pepys was more apt in learning than how to make money safely and cleanly. Mr. Yeabsley, who stopped by the next day, settled with him in his private room. Their reckoning tallied and he paid Mr. Pepys two hundred pounds, "which is a great blessing," and he concluded: "The God of heaven make me thankful for it."

On January 31, 1667, Nicholas Osborne came to the navy office to get four thousand pounds in money and commercial paper for Mr. Dennis Gauden, Navy Victualler. In place of this transaction, he left an acknowledgment for forty-eight hundred pounds and told Mr. Pepys that the eight hundred pounds of unreal wealth would be divided between him and Mr. Povy. Money to the extent of eight hundred pounds cannot be conjured on paper, but Mr. Pepys knew that the reality of it would be produced from the buying and selling of victuals. On February 4, Mr. Gauden decided to give him six hundred pounds and Mr. Povy two hundred. At month's end, moreover, Mr. Pepys admitted that the interest that he had entirely lost while some of the King's money lay idle in his trunk at the navy office had been a great temptation to him, especially since things seemed currently to be generally safe in the kingdom. Dormant, unused funds could surely be invested for short terms at interest to Mr. Pepys if he could find a banker who would promise to return the funds upon short notice. There would be no reason for an amount of the King's money to lie idle in a trunk and Mr. Pepys not realize a little personal profit from it. Who could be the loser or the wiser? "Thus the month ends": he writes, "myself in very good health and content of mind in my family."

CHAPTER 4

A Man and His Family

OTHER daily activities brought Mr. Pepys in contact with his family. In his relationships with his father, mother, sister Paulina, and brothers Thomas and John Pepys, Mr. Pepys was undoubtedly the leader. He gave orders, made decisions, and treated each as a poor relative. For Father Pepys, he had the concern that a successful son often shows for a man treading the narrow ledge of failure, for Father Pepys had been a good tailor who did not know how to collect his bills, who had sought unsuccessfully at the Restoration to secure with his son's aid a place in the King's Wardrobe, and who at Mr. Pepys's insistence had taken up residence in the country at Brampton on the little estate left by his brother, Mr. Pepys's uncle, Robert, who died on July 5, 1661. Toward his quarrelsome mother, Mr. Pepys maintained a rather negative attitude. She was a shrew, to be truthful about it; and mother and son did not get along well together. He gave her pity but not much else.

Mr. Pepys's brother Tom, who had taken over the little tailoring business after the father had settled at Brampton in August, 1661, was adept with a needle; but he neglected business, his debts bore him down, and consumption killed him on March 15, 1664, in the thirtieth year of his age. His brother John (1641-1677), who showed some early signs of promise, was a Cambridge scholar; and Mr. Pepys contributed generously to keep him there. Although he disliked his shrewish sister Paulina, Mr. Pepys was a generous and a proper brother; he provided handsomely for her marriage to Mr. John Jackson by giving six hundred pounds outright for her dowry and by agreeing to a jointure for her of sixty pounds per annum. The agreement was formally signed on February 10, 1668, in Cousin Roger Pepys's chambers at Westminster Hall, and Paulina was duly married on the 27th. But Mr. Pepys did not attend the wedding.

I *The Household*

Another domestic problem, one of many in the years to come, called for firm action from Mr. Pepys. He suspected that Will—his servant, a troublesome boy and a rogue—was a thief. Suspecting that he had stolen a letter containing half a crown that a Mr. Jenkins had left at the house on August 28, 1660, to be sent to his son, Mr. and Mrs. Pepys, next morning, questioned the young culprit who faced them down with confidence and clever denials. Later that day, Mrs. Pepys thought that she had discovered further evidence of his pilfering when she discovered in the place Mr. Pepys euphemistically calls "the house of office" a sixpenny piece that Will had stolen from Clerk Will Hewer's closet. When Will's bad behavior continued, the Pepyses discharged him.

Servant problems were just beginning, however. Jane Wayneman was already working for the Pepyses, and her brother, more troublesome even than Will, and bearing the same name, came to work for them on September 21. Seeing him next morning, Mr. Pepys thought him "a pretty, well-looked boy." Good-looking though he may have been, he gave Mr. Pepys "the very devil"; he had to thrash him again and again for lying, fighting, and sassing Father Pepys and Mrs. Pepys. Mr. Pepys finally turned him away on July 7, 1663, and would not re-employ him despite Jane's tearful pleadings.

Although a pleasant person, Jane Wayneman had a mind of her own and quaint whimsical country ways. Like any good servant, she could be stubborn and cheeky on occasion; for she was a person, not a pushover. Alone in the house on August 1, 1662, on account of Mrs. Pepys's being in the country, and disappointed that Sir William Penn's maid, Betty, was also not in the city, Mr. Pepys had "a mind to my own wench"; but, cautious man that he was, he confesses that "I dare not for fear she should prove honest, and refuse and then tell my wife." Although he had had a bad "hangover" and had been vomiting in the basin, he had eyed Jane at an earlier and more innocent time when she had amused the Pepyses by "running up and down so innocently in her smock. . . ." The thought of "a bout" with Jane pricked him often during this lonely spell at his lodgings. On

August 6, 1662, he confided that he could hardly keep his mind off her, but he was really afraid of the thorny housemaid. A self-righteous thought led him away from temptation: he hoped he would not "fall to such a shame" to himself; but he was not sure if she would lie with him. A sassy, brawling, rough-and-ready country wench who went from bad to worse, she finally left the Pepyses early in February, 1663. It was a tearful leave-taking, for Mr. Pepys had a real fondness for the lusty young termagant. She visited the Pepyses on July 28 to entreat Mr. Pepys to hire Will again, but he was through with the Waynemans even though Jane's name was mentioned favorably in the future.

The servant problem plagued Mr. Pepys constantly, bothered his conscience, and upset his morals. To add to his irritation, moreover, that forward clerk, Will Hewer, had developed a bad habit of keeping his hat on in the house; he did not pay proper respect in general to his master and to Mrs. Pepys; but in other ways he was a rather good worker. Mrs. Pepys, moreover, could not manage servants well because there was a quality about her that induced familiarity from both menservants and maidservants. On October 30, 1661, Mr. Pepys mused that increased fortune was an inconvenience; it obliged a man to keep troublesome servants. At a future time, a servant almost wrecked his home and may have hastened Mrs. Pepys's untimely death by heartbreak, so upset was she in finding Mr. Pepys in an inextricable position with a servant, Deborah Willett. And various servants troubled his heart and his household after Elizabeth's death, for he did not risk a second marriage.

It would be a mistake to assume that in his living quarters in Seething Lane all was well ordered. Although Mrs. Pepys tried her best, she was, truth to tell, a bad housekeeper; and bad housekeepers never improve by merely moving into fine houses. To make matters worse, she kept a dog that had even less respect than had Mrs. Pepys for her surroundings. Mr. Pepys, who occasionally uses fine words to report foul habits, accused the animal on November 6 of "fouling the house." When he demanded that the bitch be kept in the cellar, Mrs. Pepys came to the creature's defense. Although Mr. Pepys claimed that he would have his will, dogs and wives can be singularly unimpressed by manpower; and he did not quite say who prevailed. He reports: "And so we went to bed and lay all night in a quarrel. This night

I was troubled all night with a dream that my wife was dead, which made me that I slept ill all night." One may safely guess that if the bitch were banished to the cellar that night, she had quietly regained her place upstairs.

One of Mr. Pepys's numberless quarrels with his wife erupted on October 24, 1660, this time for hiding half-a-crown of his money in a paper box somewhere and forgetting where. But always quick to forgive and forget his wife's shortcomings, he says that "we were friends again as we are always." His good will toward Mrs. Pepys took a considerable turn later in the morning when Captain Murford put three pounds in his hand for a kindness that Mr. Pepys had done him. He would not take the gift then; he told Murford to keep it until he had enough to buy Mrs. Pepys a necklace.

The New Year Day of 1662 did not begin propitiously, for Mr. Pepys records that, waking this morning suddenly out of sleep, he did with his elbow hit his wife a great blow over her face and nose which awakened her with pain but that he was sorry and fell asleep again. This blow was, no doubt, an accident; and, in all fairness to him, it must be said that Mr. Pepys found it necessary to lay hands upon Elizabeth only a time or two during their marriage.

The modern habit of the daily bath may be a commendable one, but it was not practiced in the Pepys household. It must have been an inconvenient process at best, involving jars and lavers and having to go forward in the scullery, or worse, in the house of office. We know that Mr. Pepys washed parts of himself occasionally: feet, head . . . and that he deodorized himself sometimes with plug tobacco; but Mrs. Pepys, as the phrase goes, was something else. On February 21, 1665, with her maid attending, she went, however, to a hot-house to bathe herself. Proud of herself and feeling superior, Mrs. Pepys would not suffer her husband to sleep in the bed with her, and he was cold all night. She bragged a little about the ablution to Mr. Pepys and pretended to a resolution of being hereafter very clean. Knowing her, Mr. Pepys adds, "How long it will hold I can guess." Her resolution to cleanliness lasted at least three days, for on Saturday night, February 25, he records this fact: "at night late home, and to clean myself with warm water; my wife will have me, because she do herself, and so to bed."

II *Mr. Pepys Loses His Temper*

Drawn taut by labyrinthine turns of business, Mr. Pepys's nerve strings snapped on December 19, 1664. He blacked Mrs. Pepys's eye and was thoroughly ashamed of himself for having had to do it. It was a small matter, hardly worth mentioning, that triggered the blow. He had had to reprimand her for her poor household management, but she had talked back to him and he had clouted her: "I did strike her over her left eye such a blow as the poor wretch did cry out and was in great pain, but yet her spirit was such as to endeavour to bite and scratch me. . . ." What is a poor man to do under such circumstances? Mr. Pepys, the prudent one, knew; for, "coying with her," he made her stop crying and then sent for butter and parsley, presumably to make a poultice. She laid something to her eye all day, and the servants noticed it.

After this Sunday-night misunderstanding with his wife, he went about his usual official business next morning, meeting with the Duke, Mr. Coventry, Sir George Carteret, and Commissioners Minnes and Batten. An appointment, too, with Mrs. Bagwell found that good lady in no mood for love, and Mr. Pepys was vexed with her. But Mrs. Pepys, despite an obvious black eye, was pleased with him when he returned home. Daily relationships between Mr. Pepys and his wife, though reasonable enough, were subject to sudden outbursts of peevishness or anger. Still another instance came on May 11, 1667, when Mrs. Pepys put on a blonde wig. The Pepyses were on the way to Tower Hill with company in the coach, and he waited until the return journey to lay down the law to her. Making a fist he swore "by God" several times and declared that he would not endure her folly. Impressed and taken off guard, Mrs. Pepys said nothing; he went to his office, came home late, and without his supper went to bed vexed. By next morning, Sunday, Mr. Pepys had a right to expect that his wife would be humble and remorseful and would seek his forgiveness, as a proper wife should. He might have achieved a moral victory, but he pressed his advantage a little too far, and he records how Mrs. Pepys exploded: "by and by down comes my wife to me in her nightgown and we began calmly, that upon having money to lace her gown for second mourning, she would promise to wear white locks no more in my sight, which I, like a severe fool, thinking not enough, begun to except against, and made her fly out to very high terms and cry, and in her heart told me of keeping company with Mrs. Knipp [*sic*] saying, that if I would promise never to see her more of whom she hath more reason to suspect than I had heretofore of Pembleton, she would never wear white locks more." This bargaining—this having to submit to an ultimatum—made him angry, but husbandly cautious wisdom helped him save face. He restrained himself, inwardly resolved that he would stop seeing Mrs. Knepp,[1] and gave his wife money for lace; and she promised to wear no more white locks while he lived. They were soon as good friends as ever, and he celebrated the occasion by taking her to a French restaurant of which Monsieur Robins, the wigmaker, was proprietor.

Lest the reader think that Mr. Pepys was a perfect man, let him be reminded that he had quite average human failures; among these was jealousy. On January 10, 1661, for instance, leaving Mrs. Pepys to dine at Mrs. Hunt's while he went to Lady Montagu's for his dinner, he returned and found a lodger there, a flattering Frenchman, taking a quick kiss of Mrs. Pepys, "which I did not like, though there could not be any hurt in it." Mr. Pepys was not an overwhelmingly jealous man, but neither was he altogether trusting. There were times when buxom, high-spirited Mrs. Pepys caused him to open doors suddenly, to sit silently listening, or to inspect his bed to see if she had used it lately and for what purpose. The young couple, however, were devoted to each other; and, despite the frequent marital squalls, the decade or so that they spent together witnessed a well-spiced union.

Although Mrs. Pepys never speaks in the *Diary*, the reader knows quite well what she was like. She could bristle her husband's ears with squawking; and she could tantalize him, make him jealous, and demand a *quid pro quo* for the balm of uxorial consolations. She liked to dress in the latest fashions, and Mr. Pepys sometimes had to object to her ruffles and laces. Above all else, she was, as has been noted, a dreadful housekeeper; and the *Diary* bears frequent witness to her cluttered habits. Her husband, however, beat and kicked a slatternly housemaid if his house were not handsome when he wanted it to be. Mrs. Pepys herself was often too frowzy, and he frequently had to be angry with her for the arm's length at which he found it necessary to stay from her. On January 11, 1661, and there were other instances much worse, he was discontented at dinner time that she was not "neater now she has two maids."

III *Uncle Robert Pepys's Illness and Death*

When a letter from Brampton, on June 26, 1661, informed Mr. Pepys that Uncle Robert was seriously ill with a dizziness in his head, Mr. Pepys expressed a pious wish, in a spirit of resignation, that God's will be done; for Father Pepys had told him recently that Uncle Robert had promised to make Mr. Pepys his heir. Uncle Robert's wife had written to ask Father Pepys to come to Brampton to look after things. In a father-and-son conversation, Mr. Pepys suggested next day that his father tell Uncle Robert that he intended to buy land at Brampton; he would pay as much as six hundred pounds ready money and one hundred fifty pounds a year to make up as much as would buy an income of fifty pounds annually. This discussion with ailing Uncle Robert would, of course, lead him to think that the Clerk of the Acts was worth more than he actually was, for at this date he was not worth more than five hundred pounds ready money. Mr. Battersby, the apothecary, told Mr. Pepys on July 4 that he would bet his life that bleeding by leeches would cure Uncle Robert's piles; but Mr. Pepys resolved not to meddle with whatever therapy was being followed. Indeed, he need not have been concerned, for Uncle Robert died the next day. Hearing the news, Mr. Pepys admitted that he was sorry in some respect, but he added that he was "glad in my expectations in another."

Preparing to leave for Brampton the next day, July 6, he bought a new pair of boots in St. Martin's and left with the messenger who had brought the news. When he reached Brampton and found that Uncle Robert's body had been placed by the chimney in the hall and had begun to smell, the young autocrat ordered the corpse placed in the yard all night with two men to watch it. The funeral was held in fine country disorder; and, being on Sunday, it attracted a large crowd. The custom of providing refreshments for all put the Pepyses to great shift, but they gave the mourners what they had of wine and other things. The Reverend Mr. John Turner preached a plausible enough sermon in which he specified little concerning the deceased but that he was one so well known for his honesty that his reputation spoke for him.

Mr. Pepys fared well enough in the will which stated that he should inherit the Brampton property at the death of his father. Uncle Robert's estate turned out to be much less than people had thought, his papers were in a frightful tangle, and various relatives entered caveats and threatened lawsuits, since Uncle Robert had not left them anything. It took painful years of litigious hauling and pulling before Mr. Samuel Pepys held a clear title to Uncle Robert's modest estate.

Although the estate was minuscule in contrast to his expectation, the Clerk of the Acts informed his colleagues and underlings that the estate left him an income of two hundred a year besides ready cash. He did so "Because I would put an esteem upon myself," he admitted; he knew that nothing so raises a man in the esteem of others as their suspicion that he is, secretly, in good financial circumstances. He found it necessary, though, to speak sharply to his mother who had recently gone on a spending spree in anticipation of the new riches from the estate of her brother-in-law.

IV *Mr. Pepys's Kinfolk*

Mr. Pepys spent a part of many typical days with his relatives. In his upward climb, however, he got no help whatever from these kinfolk; indeed, they seemed always about to pull him down. A more miscellaneous assortment of plain, Puritan folk could hardly be found. How could a man become a courtier or be dubbed knight with such relatives as brother Tom, Uncle Fenner, and Uncle Wight, a fishmonger and his father's half brother? These neighboring relatives, a scurvy crowd, brought to the surface Mr. Pepys's snobbishness and what he had of complexes and frustrations. Uncle Fenner, the blacksmith, whose wife had died on August 19, 1661, and who, on October 31, Mr. Pepys had found "youthsome" and drinking at the tavern, had substantiated Pepys's guess that he would remarry; and his bride was also quite below Mr. Pepys's standards.

Family concerned him, of course, from day to day. During his visit on July 18, 1660, to the Earl of Sandwich, someone had delivered half a buck from the family estate at Hinchingbroke. The buck had gone gamey "and it smelling a little strong my Lord did give it to me (though it was as good as any could be)."

The gamey meat provided a good occasion to visit his parents; he took it to his mother "to dispose of as she pleased." Father Pepys was not at home, and his son was gratified at the temporary surcease from the pressure to which his father was currently subjecting him to secure a job at His Majesty's Wardrobe. Mr. Pepys was worried on August 28, 1660, about his "poor mother," and expressed the fear that she would not last long; but she fooled him and lived until 1667.

V *The Dancing Master*

On April 24, 1663, Mr. Pepys sent the houseboy to inquire of two dancing masters that the little fellow had told him about, for he would teach Mrs. Pepys to dance. If Mr. Pepys could have known what wrenches of jealous anxiety the new dancing master would cause, he surely would not have hired him. Mr. Pembleton began on April 25 to teach Mrs. Pepys the new steps and there was incidental merry laughter at *pas* and *faux pas*. Mrs. Pepys did well enough but suffered from the oafish conceit of the awkward beginner, and Mr. Pepys was a little bit peeved with her.

Entering himself as a pupil for dancing lessons on May 4 cost Mr. Pepys ten shillings. At the prodding of Mrs. Pepys and the dancing master he learned the mincing steps of the coranto, and consoled himself that the dance was a thing very useful for a gentleman and that he might have occasion to use it. Evidence of his Puritan conscience and its cost in money lies in Mr. Pepys's paying fifteen shillings into the poor box for indulging in the frivolity of dancing lessons.

It was not long before Mr. Pembleton, unbidden by Mr. Pepys, took to "pop-calling." These visits, suspiciously timed to coincide with the master's absence from the house, continued for months and reduced Mr. Pepys to an unseemly fidgety paroxism unbecoming to a city man and to such an important person as the Clerk of the Acts. Mrs. Pepys was the type of wife who got out of hand easily; for, if Mr. Pepys allowed her a privilege or two, or provided a little outlet or relaxation, she quickly became forward and neglected her wifely duties. She put him at his wit's end, and Mr. Pembleton seemed to fortify her courage. On May 21, she actually talked back to her husband when he brought up the matter of the dancing. So sharply did she put him in his place that he resolved to fine himself 2/6 every time he mentioned the dancing again; but, by Goodness, he would terminate the lessons at month's end.

Pembleton continued to be in and out of the house, Mr. Pepys participated in the dancing, and the activity was tiring and sometimes made him late for work. At supper, Mrs. Pepys used the word "devil"; but he would not brook such a word, and forbade her to use it again. She then upbraided him scornfully in the presence of the maid, Mary Ashwell "and the rest of the world," and he complained: "I know not now-a-days how to check [her], as I would heretofore, for less than that would have made me strike her. So that I fear without great discretion I shall go near to lose my command over her, and nothing do it more than giving her this occasion of dancing and other pleasures, whereby her mind is taken up from her business and finds other sweets besides pleasing of me, and so makes her that she begins not at all to take pleasure in me or study to please me as heretofore."

On Sunday, May 24, he took one of Dr. Hollyard's pills for constipation and did not go to church in the morning. Having learned that a pretty woman had been with Margaret Penn at the morning service, Mr. Pepys decided to go to church in the afternoon to look at her. What he got for his pains was a jealous seizure, for the dancing master, Mr. Pembleton, was present; and Mr. Pepys, glancing nervously at him, caught him leering at Mrs. Pepys and her curtsying quickly to him without, first, getting her husband's consent. He had noticed, too, that, no churchwoman, she had prodded him to take her to St. Olave's both forenoon and afternoon on two succeeding Sundays.

During the following days, May 26-27, he behaved in a most unseemly manner, wracked and wrenched in a perfect fit of jealousy. Odds and ends of circumstantial evidence convinced him that Mrs. Pepys's dealings with Mr. Pembleton went much deeper than dancing. He snooped, peeped, eavesdropped, and worked himself into a lather of anxiety; he simply could not keep his mind on his beloved facts and figures at the office. When he went home suddenly, Pembleton and Mrs. Pepys were, sure enough, alone in the house. Taking a busy turn or two, and uttering a loud ahem, he called to someone about a business matter, left the house in bustling haste but doubled back, consoling himself in specious rumination that, if they had any intention of hurt, he had prevented their doing anything at that time. He was rendered even more suspicious by Mr. Pembleton's calling out before him to Mrs. Pepys that he could not stay and that he could not give her a dancing lesson since Mary Ashwell was out of the house. Such damned, sly cheek caused Mr. Pepys to condescend to a little bit of detective work "to see whether any of the beds were out of order or no. . . ." And, when Mrs. Pepys came upstairs to discuss household business, he inferred pure impudence in her. His discontent and suspicion followed him into restless slumber.

Getting up at three o'clock, before day, to make noisy water, he awakened Mrs. Pepys and went into an act of distraction to test what her reaction would be. When he jumped up from the bed, Mrs. Pepys put a wifely hand on him and asked the cause of his fidgetiness. He accused her of infidelity the day before, and she countered that his old disease of jealousy was flaring up again. Reproofs and denials were exchanged, but Mr. Pepys finally pampered his anxieties by believing that "her freedom with him [Pembleton] is very great and more than was convenient, but with no evil intent." In such ticklish situations a caress was easily bought, and Mrs. Pepys added tears to pacify him; for, in tight spots involving men or money, she managed him quite well.

What with his anxieties about Pembleton, it is understandable that Mr. Pepys, while strolling on the rainy spring day of May 29, 1663, took two turns forward and backward through Fleet Alley to see a couple of pretty wenches who stood at the doors there. And, God forgive him, he confessed, he could scarcely stay himself from going into their houses with them. He blamed his nature for being so apt to evil once he had turned to pleasure such as he had been having of late with dancing. He concluded that he had to impute his mental disarray to his uneasiness about his wife.

Much cloud and little sunshine filled the following days. He found, on returning from a late session at the office on June 3, that the boy was out of the house and that Mrs. Pepys was quite evasive in accounting for his absence. Every little circumstance reminded Mr. Pepys of the dancing master, and he concluded that she had sent the boy to him with a message. Restless the long night through, he awakened next morning with Pembleton on his mind. "Up betimes, and my wife and Ashwell and I whiled away the morning up and down while they got themselves ready, and I did so watch to see my wife put on drawers, which poor soul she did, and yet I could not get off my suspicions, she having a mind to go into Fenchurch Street before she went out for good and all with me, which I must needs construe to be to meet Pembleton. . . ." He gained a measure of tentative reassurance when Mrs. Pepys told him afterward that she had been seeking to buy a fan in Fenchurch Street and did not want him to know of the transaction.

Sunday, June 7, was an uneasy culmination to the previous week. Mr. Pepys enjoyed lying abed with his wife on a morning, especially a Sunday morning, while talking over the comfortable trivia of home and office and, no doubt, settling with firm *obiter dicta* every other man's affairs. This morning, though, the subject of discussion abed, sometimes in anger, was their own brittle relationships. Reaching a tentative truce, he went to church where he slept soundly through the sermons, morning and afternoon. Later he fell again to malevolent spatting with his wife, this time over the weighty difference concerning whose servant boy was the prettier, his or Sir William Penn's; Mrs. Pepys supported the claims of their own lad; he peevishly denied them. "It troubles me to see that every small thing is enough now-a-days to bring a difference between us," he complained, making the old discovery about man and wife that, when circumstances go awry, they can get on each other's nerves.

On Monday, he reported that after dinner they had "a little jangling . . ." in the presence of the maid, Mary Ashwell; and Mrs. Pepys had called him a liar. She had taken up the habit of "facing him out" in the maid's presence; she thought, said he, that in Ashwell's presence he would not say or do anything of force to her. He was quite distressed that he had allowed her such freedom lately that she had developed such a low boiling point. In sheer frustration he retired to his chamber to leaf through a concordance of the Bible.

Having to suffer another visit from Mr. Pembleton the next night added to Mr. Pepys's discomfort; it aroused his suspicion that this visit might be in fulfillment of a promise to call once before Mrs. Pepys left for Brampton, Mr. Pepys having decided to send her there for a vacation. He admitted Mr. Pembleton, treated him with cold courtesy, but permitted him to go upstairs to dance with Mrs. Pepys, Mary Ashwell attending. The scraping and shuffling on the floor above his head reassured him; but, when the measure came to a halt, he put his ear to the door. Mr. Pembleton, reassuringly, did not overstay his time; and Mr. Pepys wrung a little consolation from the knowledge that he would soon put distance between Mr. Pembleton and Mrs. Pepys. She left for Brampton, thank Goodness, on Monday, June 15.

Facing his wife, who returned to London on August 12, 1663, he found her strange. Not knowing what mood she expected him to be in, he resorted to kind words, a wise way to resume their marriage. Mrs. Pepys, on her part, complained about the maid, Mary Ashwell, and about the ill-usage of her by his family at Brampton. Knowing that she was as much at fault as anyone, he decided not to pry too deeply into the fractious circumstances at Brampton.

On the following day, Mr. Pepys spoke to Mrs. Harper, his friend the coffeehouse keeper, about her relative Jane Gentleman, and arranged that she should join his household as chambermaid. Knowing Mrs. Pepys's stubbornness, he was resigned to dismissing the charming, talented Mary Ashwell; and he drew cold comfort from the thought that a housemaid would cost less than a companion for Mrs. Pepys. The plucky little Mary would not be dismissed, however, without stating her side of the case; and that evening she accused Mrs. Pepys in his presence. Even in reporting this painful situation, Mr. Pepys is at his best. He stated that he perceived that she had received most base usage from his wife, which his wife sillily denied; but it was impossible the wench could so particularly invent words and actions against which his wife had nothing to say and which she could only flatly deny. Mr. Pepys learned, moreover, that they had come to blows and had used high words even at Hinchingbroke House among Lady Sandwich's servants, and Mr. Pepys was mightily ashamed to learn of this tumult. He said nothing to either Mrs. Pepys or Mary Ashwell, but let them talk until the girl left them abed; then he spoke his mind to his wife "with great sobriety of grief, and so to sleep." The subject of Mary Ashwell began the next day, and stubborn Elizabeth Pepys would not relent; she was determined to carry off the charges against the girl, and her husband became convinced that she had to be dismissed. Mary left the Pepys's household on August 25.

He and Mrs. Pepys had a serious row on November 2, 1663, when she accused Jane Gentleman of lying. Because of constant trouble with the servants, he was usually disposed to silence his wife's frequent accusations; but she was not, as has been noted, the kind of wife to be shushed. She could buck and bridle at him, and did. On this occasion she called him perfidious, lacking in courage, and what not; and Mr. Pepys recorded that, although he would charge some of the outburst to temper, some of her words represented what she thought of him. He revealed the outcome of the quarrel, reporting that he tempered himself very well so that, although they went to bed in discontent, she yielded to him and began to be fond and that, before they went to sleep, they had become very good friends. As a husband, Mr. Samuel Pepys came close to virtue: he was generous, humorous, playful; occasionally assertive, he was quick to back down in an argument and, withal, was kind and obedient to his wife, especially when she was femininely pettish and unreasonable.

Tenderhearted Mr. Pepys was moved almost to tears during Dr. Hollyard's professional visit to Mrs. Pepys, November 16-18. She insisted that she would allow no one else, even the maids, to be in attendance when the surgeon operated for her malady, which Mr. Pepys describes: "her great conflux of humours, heretofore that did use to swell there, which in breaking left a hollow which has since gone in further and further, till now it is near three inches deep, but as God would have it do not run into the bodyward but keeps to the outside of the skin, and so he must be forced to cut it open all along. . . ." Although this sebaceous cyst was benign and although the maids were easily led to believe that it was the piles, Mrs. Pepys was, understandably, reluctant to give them occasion to discourse about it. The operation was not necessary, after all, said the surgeon; a poultice causing fomentation would prove efficacious. And Mr. Pepys's mind was greatly relieved; he could not have stood, he admitted, to see his wife cut in his presence.

A hypochondriac like Mr. Pepys would not miss such a good chance, his wife's maladies so much in evidence, to develop a sympathetic illness of his own. "I had great discourse with him about my disease," he announced portentously. The manly regimen that Dr. Hollyard proposed, efficacious and reasonable enough for anyone in any age, was, in the morning, some loosening gruel; at night roasted apples, now and then wine with the dinner; bread and butter and honey and rye bread if his system could endure such loosening foods; a clyster once a week with honey now and then instead of butter. The fact that, on November 18, when Dr. Hollyard arrived to give Mrs. Pepys professional care, he was suspiciously talkative was not at all reassuring to Mr. Pepys, who thought that he had had a drink or two. The doctor's talk was full of Latin and of discourse about Calvin and Luther.

VI   *Uncle Wight, Seducer*

Uncle Wight, of all people, gave Mr. Pepys real cause for concern. He was the type of goatish elder relative who presumed upon family good will and who also felt and kissed the women behind doors, making a nuisance and a general fool of himself to the great embarrassment of all concerned. Mr. Pepys's reaction to Uncle Wight's advances upon Mrs. Pepys was surprising, to say the least. When Mr. Pepys learned that Uncle Wight, while enjoying the hospitality of his home at dinner and cards on January 12, 1664, had accosted Mrs. Pepys, had hoped that she was with child, had kissed her earnestly, and had told her he should be very glad of it, Mr. Pepys rationalized that, from all circumstances, Uncle Wight had intentions to do them some good. Some intention of good, Uncle Wight did indeed have: if Mr. Pepys could not father a child, Uncle Wight could and would; and, after much hemming and hawing, he offered Mrs. Pepys five hundred pounds to provide Mr. Pepys an heir. At first Mr. Pepys was unwilling to entertain any thought of being cuckolded, even after Uncle Wight, on January 15, had visited Mrs. Pepys and questioned her closely about pregnancy. To Uncle Wight's groping, Mr. Pepys reports this temporizing reaction "which makes me wonder what his meaning is, and after all my thoughts, I cannot think, unless it be in order to the making his will, that he might know how to do by me, and I would to God my wife had told him that she was." Uncle Wight, of course, had another end in mind. Whatever the connection may have been with this thorny problem, a visit to Betty Lane seemed fitting to Mr. Pepys the following day. An account of his session with Betty is best hidden by suspension points, and Mr. Pepys records it in dog-French: "So home to supper and to bed, with my mind un peu troubled pour ce que fait today, but I hope it will be la dernier de toute ma vie." It was, nevertheless, not his last visit.

As Uncle Wight continued to press his strange suit to Mrs. Pepys, his position became increasingly untenable. Whenever he could catch her alone, he told her that he loved her but that it was inconvenient for obvious reasons to show his love openly. Mr. Pepys accurately interpreted his uncle's wish for secrecy, but what he persistently misinterpreted was his motive. Mr. Pepys continued to think that Uncle Wight meant them well and wanted to give them something if he should die without children. Disclosing what he really had in mind for Mrs. Pepys, Uncle Wight proposed: "had she a child it should be his heir." To this ambiguous statement, he added another: should she or Mr. Pepys want, he would be their friend; and the aging seducer instructed Mrs. Pepys to appease Aunt Wight always for she was a pettish woman. When Mrs. Pepys told her husband what had transpired, Mr. Pepys, almost willfully, it seems, missed the point: "which argues a design I think he has of keeping us in with his wife in order to our good sure."

Aunt Wight, in the meantime, confided in Mrs. Pepys and revealed a different set of circumstances in regard to her husband's generous talk: Uncle Wight had promised to double the portion to his own wife at his death as a jointure. Moreover, he had given one hundred pounds to her niece, Mary, and had named her to a good legacy at his death and had also done as much for Aunt Wight's other niece. Hearing this news, Mr. Pepys was vexed; and the reader of the *Diary* can imagine the uneasy stirrings in his mind: was the game worth the candle to put Mrs. Pepys forward as bait to a man like Uncle Wight who made so many promises to so many females? "I will endeavour to remedy it for the time to come," was the doubtful tentative resolution that he made.

Uncle Wight had been hemming, hawing, and hinting for months; but finally he revealed his plan to Mrs. Pepys on May 11, 1664. They were both childless, he said, and then he proceeded with masterful logic to propose that they fall to the business, jointly, of producing an heir. For her participation in the proceedings he would give her in advance five hundred pounds, in either money or jewels; and he would make the child his heir. He praised her body and offered the opinion in a sort of counterfeit laughing way that, for all he knew, the entire business would be lawful. Mrs. Pepys gave him a "very warm answer" of such a nature that he did not withdraw the offer or say that he was jesting but simply that, since he noticed that she did not have a mind to accept the proposal, he would say no more to her of it; but he did ask her not to repeat what he had said. Mrs. Pepys sent to the office for her husband to come quickly to hear this development; and, when she told him of Uncle Wight's offer, he was confused and disappointed. He was determined, nevertheless, to say nothing to Uncle Wight until he could figure out his uncle's actions. Well, said Mr. Pepys, it was plain that Uncle Wight was in dead earnest; but he feared that, for all of that worthy's kindness, he was motivated by lust for Mrs. Pepys.

VII *Mother Pepys Dies*

On March 26, 1667, brother John Pepys had written from Brampton to say that he had actually heard the death rattle in his mother's throat and that Father Pepys was likely to die of grief. Human nature led Mr. Pepys to thank God, even in this sad state of affairs, for his own good health and well-being. Next day when he learned of his mother's death, Mr. Pepys observed the signs of grief, "weeping heartily" when he learned that Mother Pepys's dying words were, "God bless my poor Sam." He was soon at ease in mind—enough to attend to the outward symbols of grief in his customary business-like way by purchasing items of mourning such as hoods, scarfs, and gloves to send to his country relations and for his own London household.

On Sunday morning, March 31, Mr. Pepys records: "Up, and my tailor's boy brings my mourning clothes home, and my wife hers and Baker's, but they go not to church this morning. I to church, and with my mourning, very handsome, and new periwigg, make a great shew." Betty Michell and her husband visited after church, but the young wife was so great with child that Mr. Pepys could scarcely conceal his discomfiture; he exclaimed that he loved her and ever would but that the "poor wretch" was almost ready to lie down. By May 4, Mr. Pepys seemed to have quite forgotten his grief for his mother's death; and he had not attended the funeral. He mentions, though, that one of the wigs that he had "cheapened" for the mourning period was full of nits as, in fact, were so many of Jervas the barber's wigs. The expense incurred by his mother's funeral was among the two or three things that vexed him on April 3.

VIII   *Mr. Pepys in Serious Trouble*

If the *Diary* had closed with the entry of Lord's Day, October 25, 1668, it would have ended with one of the finest stories of all. But it also would have ended with curtains sadly, if decently, drawn on the activities of Mr. Pepys; but such an ending is not the case. He went on, even in the *Diary*, to enjoy daily, or almost daily, wonders and delights and to become increasingly important in the later years, and to record in other, but dull, journals, his rise in the busy world about him. To come slowly and reluctantly to the story, and to use a mixed modern metaphor, the roof caved in on him the night of October 25:

and, after supper, to have my head combed by Deb, which occasioned the greatest sorrow to me that ever I knew in this world, for my wife coming up suddenly, did find me embracing the girl. . . . I was at a wonderful loss upon it, and the girle also, and I endeavoured to put it off, but my wife was struck mute and grew angry, and so her voice come to her, grew quite out of order, and I to say little, but to bed, and my wife said little also, but could not sleep all night, but about two in the morning waked me and cried, and fell to tell me as a great secret that she was a Roman Catholique . . . which troubled me, . . . but she went on from one thing to another till at last it appeared plainly her trouble was at what she saw, but yet I did not know how much she saw, and therefore said nothing to her.

Mrs. Pepys reproached him until almost morning for his inconstancy and for preferring "a sorry girl" above her; and she also told Mr. Pepys, to his great sorrow, that she would turn the little girl out of doors.

When his wife told him on November 13 that Deb had found another job and would leave the next day, Mr. Pepys shows just how contrite he was for his recent misconduct with her by recording in his *Diary* that the information troubled him: "and the truth is, I have a good mind to have the maidenhead of this girl. . . ." He was unable to fulfill this ambition, however, for Mrs. Pepys shielded him from Deb. She did not even allow him to hand the girl her wages; and, when he objected a little to this insult to his manhood and to his honesty, she instantly flew into a rage, called him dog and rogue, and said that he had a rotten heart. Well should she have watched her husband; for, although he bore her accusations with manly patience, he wrapped forty shillings in paper to slip into Deb's hands.

The search for Deb went on apace for she had seemed to be hiding from Mr. Pepys in the crooked lanes of the city and in its suburbs. Mrs. Pepys, meantime, showed him no mercy; her incessant recrimination and an occasional blow and hair pulling reduced her husband to pleas for forgiveness and sometimes to tears. She got him to agree to accept Will Hewer as a constant bodyguard, but Mr. Pepys occasionally slipped away from his good-natured clerk and was repaid with a quick glance or by a furtive meeting with Deb. But he failed at last to make any real contact with her.

The coach that Mr. Pepys had bought finally arrived on November 30, 1668, and he stated proudly that his wife "went the first time abroad to take the maidenhead of her coach." A fine pair of black coach-horses costing fifty pounds was delivered to him on December 12. A portent of tragedy followed next day, Sunday: "In the night my wife, very ill, vomited . . .," he reports. Despite an occasional unpleasantness, Mr. Pepys's days were good ones, the ladies frequently supplying diversions.

CHAPTER 5

Mr. Pepys and the Ladies

THE reputation of Mr. Pepys as a lady's man is generally over-drawn, for he was a bashful and cautious man; and, with the exception of a conquest here and there of a barmaid, a servant girl, or the wife of a sailor at sea, his married life was one of more or less steady devotion to the buxom Elizabeth. Discreet flirtations were many, the squeeze of a hand there, the nibbling of a finger of a glove there, and an ambiguous thrust yonder summarize many of his amours. He could hem and haw for years in the presence of Betty Michell whom he called "my other wife" or the frisky actress Mrs. Knepp before finally, if at all, finding courage to make love to either of them. Timid, cautious, busy little Mr. Pepys simply did not fit the mould of the aggressive gallant in which he is often cast in the popular mind.

Among his escapades is a typical furtive encounter with a lady, who later became an intimate friend, that took place on Sunday, August 12, 1660. Mr. Pepys had attended Whitehall Chapel and had heard a good sermon by the Reverend Edmund Calamy, as well as a brave anthem composed and sung by Captain Henry Cooke.[1] The King and everybody were pleased. Mr. Pepys had a good dinner at Lord Sandwich's house with the Earl's man, Mr. William Shepley: and then, in good humor, he had gone for a walk. Meeting Miss Betty Lane of Westminster Hall, he took her back to his Lordship's house, His Lordship being at the Lord Chamberlain's for dinner, and gave her a bottle of wine in the garden. Mr. Fairbrother of Cambridge came upon the couple, but Mr. Pepys quite sociably got him to take a drink too. "After that," says Mr. Pepys, "I took her to my house, where I was exceeding free in dallying with her, and she not unfree to take it."

Engaging in frequent dialogues with his conscience, Mr. Pepys put his knowledge of foreign tongues to use to record his encounters with the ladies. Frances Tooker, daughter to the messenger at the navy office, was a frequent recipient of his attentions. He did what he would with her, a mere girl, on June 7, 1666; and he pursued her through nubility and beyond to the time when he reported on February 24, 1667, that she had an unmentionable malady. He reported, nevertheless, "ego had opportunity para baiser her . . ." on March 15. Of gentle Mrs. Bagwell at Deptford, he reports, on February 20, 1665, "entrer en la maison de la femme Bagwell . . . neanmoins en fin j'avais ma volonte de elle. . . ." And, when Mrs. Daniel called on May 23, 1667, to seek a job for her husband, Mr. Pepys, leaving his wife and father upstairs, reports the encounter: "je was ashamed de peur that my people pensait to pragma de it." When upon his return home, Mrs. Pepys noticed his discomfiture, he explained, "car ego was in much chaleur et de body and of animi, which I put off with the heat of the season . . . but I had some fear hung upon me lest alcuno had sidi decouvert." His spring heat still upon him, Mr. Pepys engaged in a shocking encounter with otherwise unidentified "Mrs. Pen" this same day and boasted: "This afternoon I had opportunity para jouer with Mrs. Pen, tokendo her mammailles and baisando elle, being sola in the casa of her pater, and she fort willing."

But a chilling experience was his lot on August 5, 1663, when Lady Jemimah Montagu came upon him unawares at the Parliament Stairs while he was leading Miss Lane by the hand. Kindly Lady Jem appeared not to notice, but Mr. Pepys's session with Miss Lane was nigh ruined by his indecision whether or not to engross Her Ladyship in conversation in hope against hope that she hadn't seen him. His anxieties to the contrary notwithstanding, he took Miss Lane to the "King's Head" where he treated her to a variety of meats and drinks, "and did so towse and handle her but could get nothing more from her . . ." though he "was very near it," and he was in such a sweat that he durst not go home by boat but took a coach.

The next day, August 6, was spent in a comparable fashion. He went to a "gossipping" at Mary Joyce's where there was much company and good cheer. "There was the King's Falconer . . . and his wife, an ugly pusse, but brought him money." Pampering his kissing-bug malady to the full with as many ladies as would permit, he backed them into corners, danced and cut capers with them, and generally felt his way.

"Great news" was his good fortune, on July 20, 1664: Betty Lane was married to one Martin; and Mr. Pepys comments that the situation there is "very fine," adding, "I must have a bout with her very shortly to see how she finds marriage." This rapscallionly, if amusing, decision he carried out the next day, July 21: "Thence to Westminster and to Mrs. Lane's lodgings, to give her joy, and there suffered me to deal with her as I hoped to do, and by and by her husband comes, a sorry, simple fellow, . . . and a sad wife I believe she will prove to him for she urged me to appoint a time as soon as he is gone out of town to give her a meeting next week."

Three days later, after he had left Mr. Coventry on July 23, 1664, Mr. Pepys found himself in "an idle and wanton humour." Walking through Fleet Alley, he saw a pretty wench at one of the doors. He passed and repassed her and finally commended himself for the sense of honor and conscience that prevented his going indoors with the young lady. He went quickly, instead, to hunt for the newlywed Mrs. Martin, whom he took across the river to an old rendezvous at Lambeth Marsh; and, as Mr. Pepys tells it, he had his pleasure of her twice. After he had finished with Mrs. Martin, Mr. Pepys's footsteps led him again to the door in Fleet Alley. Always a man of punctilious conscionableness in a tight spot, Mr. Pepys speaks: "not knowing how to command myself, and went in and there saw . . . the wickedness of these houses, and the forcing a man to present expense. The woman indeed is a most lovely woman, but I had no courage to meddle with her for fear of her not being wholesome, and so counterfeiting that I had not money enough, it was pretty to see how cunning she was, would not suffer me to have to do in any manner with her after she saw I had no money. . . ."

His wife's sojourn in the country no doubt had something to do with Mr. Pepys's frivolous inclinations. On July 25, 1664, he walked all around that end of the town "among the loathsome people and houses"; but, God be thanked, says he, he had no desire to visit any of them. The noontime entertainment next day was shared at Anthony Joyce's "gossip's dinner" to which Mr. Pepys had sent a dozen and a half bottles of wine and had paid a double share of eighteen shillings. Under certain circumstances, when alone with women who were a notch or two beneath him in social rank, Mr. Pepys could be quite "a card" with the ladies. The situation at Joyce's was just right for him, and after dinner he followed them upstairs, promptly introduced the subject of Mrs. Pepys's childlessness, and asked the ladies how he might remedy the situation. They gave him wonderfully ribald suggestions, among them not to hug his wife too hard or too much, to wear cool Holland drawers, to keep his stomach warm and his back cool, to change his positions, and "upon query whether it was best to do at night or morn, they answered me neither one nor other, but when we had most mind to it."

In order that he might not be too overdressed for a meeting with Mrs. Bagwell,[2] the business of the day of November 15, 1664, Mr. Pepys left off his "fine new cloth suit lined with plush and put on [his] poor black suit. . . ." He went to his office where there was much business, but he did little. Going to the Exchange, Mr. Pepys continues, "and thence Bagwell's wife with much ado followed me through Moorfields to a blind alehouse, and there I did caress her and eat and drink, and many hard looks and sooth the poor wretch did give me, and I think verily was troubled at what I did, but at last after many protestings by degrees I did arrive at what I would, with great pleasure, and then in the evening, it raining, walked into town to where she knew where she was, and then I took coach and to White Hall to a Committee of Tangier. . . ."

In daily thought and action Mr. Pepys kept close to the ladies. Among the miscellaneous activities of Sunday, October 21, 1666, were going to church, and then inviting Lady Penn and her daughter to dinner, attending the King and speaking of the want of money for Tangier, and reading a bit of a sermon. Then he had the pleasure of two old pastimes that he enjoyed even more: listening to a snap of gossip and meeting an easy conquest. Sir Hugh Cholmely[3] had told him that afternoon, among many other things, that Harry Killigrew[4] had been banished from the court for having said that Lady Castlemaine was a lecherous little creature when she was young. That afternoon, Pepys, even more to his delight than the gossip, had visited Mrs. Martin and met her sister, Doll, "with whom," exults Mr. Pepys, "contrary to all expectation, I did what I would, and might have done anything else."

Promise of an easy conquest always set Mr. Pepys on a busy quest to catch this or any other Doll Tearsheet who crossed his path. Betty Michell was his favorite quarry, but the little newly-wed would let him go only so far and no farther whenever he cornered her. First business for Mr. Pepys on Monday morning, October 22, was to take coach to Westminster Hall to meet her, having learned that she had spent the night at her father's house. He just missed her, but overtook her and her father and had a chance for only a greeting. The Michells had moved to new quarters; and Mr. Pepys, who managed to locate the house by next day, reported finding her alone and enjoyed her lips, "poor wretch," as much as he would. The "poor wretch" was a term of condescending affection, but Mr. Pepys may have had a little self-pity in mind when he used it. On the next day he visited the Michells, "and there find little Michell come to his new shop that he hath built there in the room of his house that was burned." Generously, Mr. Pepys adds: "I hope he will do good here." He drank and bade him joy, "for I love him and his wife well, him for his care, and her for her person." On November 1, Mr. Pepys reported that he paid Betty Michell a compliment more substantial than kisses; he sent to her by Mrs. Pepys "a very noble cake" presented him by Burton, one of the navy smiths, whose wife had baked it for Mr. Pepys, and a bottle of wine "to house-warme my Betty Michell. . . ."

A situation that might have been troublesome developed on February 1, 1667, when he went to keep an appointment with Mrs. Bagwell at Deptford. In his special brand of pre-Esperanto, Mr. Pepys revealed a part of his experience: "the mulier etait within expecting me venir. . . . By and by su marido come in, and there without any notice taken by him we discoursed of our business of getting him the new ship building by Mr. Deane, which I shall do for him." It is hard to believe that Mr. Bagwell was bargaining the ancient marital privilege for the command of a frigate. He must, instead, have been a trusting man.

When Mr. Pepys got back in town, he went in search of a more placid session. He went to Billingsgate by water and treaded his way to the "Old Swan," where, night having fallen, he took a boat to Westminster Hall to see Doll Lane. Having found her, "con elle I went to the Bell Taverne, and ibi je did do what I would con elle as well as I could, she sedendo sobre thus far and making some little resistance. But all with much content, and je tenai much pleasure cum ista." Parting from Doll, he went to his office and worked until late; thence home at last, "and merry with my wife, and to supper." Then he played, with John Pepys, a violin duet, reported this sprightly man of boundless energy and self-re-creating conscience before sleep closed his weary eyes.

The ladies made a motion on August 1, 1667, after a sorry dinner at Sir William Penn's, that Mr. Pepys escort them to the theater. Another test of the fineness of his character and disposition is that he was popular and a very pet among the ladies, for, with their ancient instinct, they could spot a kind, free-handed, fun-loving man who could flatter them with a quick kiss; a pinch on arm or buttocks; or, more distantly and circumspectly, with a glance or a secret knowing. He was good at the manners of dalliance, and given half a chance, he would go all the way with a woman. Observing that this would be the first time that he had been to the theater since the Dutch had come upon English coasts, Mr. Pepys took the ladies, presumably Mrs. Turner,[5] Mrs. Markham,[6] Mrs. Pepys and, perhaps, Lady Penn to the King's House.

At the after-theater entertainment, Mrs. Pepys's womanly intuition was at work, and she caught the signals flying between Mr. Pepys and the brassy actress, Mrs. Knepp, who always managed to make her feel uneasy; for, after all, even though it is hard to remember it, Mrs. Pepys was still a mere twenty-seven, and would understandably have felt outmaneuvered in the presence of Mrs. Knepp. Mr. Pepys reported that his wife was in the ill humor in which she always seemed to be whenever Mrs. Knepp was about, but the actress paid Mr. Pepys for her entertainment with a good story: Nell Gwynn had quit King Charles's stable and had joined Lord Buckhurst's.

Active enough at any time, Mr. Pepys was hyperactive during the summer days while Mrs. Pepys sojourned at Brampton. Since the time Mary Mercer had firmly but politely put his hand away from her thigh, Mr. Pepys had maintained an affectionate esteem for the spirited, sophisticated young woman. He had kissed her several times in the garden on January 30, 1667, under the stimulus of their own singing; but she would not hold still for his convenience. She had a good voice, looked good, and was a knowledgeable theater companion; and he was delighted that she was willing to be his partner in spending his money. When he visited Mrs. Mercer, Mary's mother, on May 12, 1668, he was a welcome guest. At Mrs. Mercer's he met "one Mrs. Susan Gayet, a very pretty black lady I never knew yet . . .," and after a little pleasant chit-chat, he took about five of the ladies for an outing, and then to an old house at Islington where they ate, drank, and sang together and were mighty merry. They went home by moonlight, and sang again in Mary Mercer's garden.

It is safe to call Mr. Pepys "a ladies' man" in the sense that he constantly needed the comfort and companionship of women. He flourished from the quiet adulation and respect that they gave him. A Sir William Penn or a Coventry could somehow cause him to feel inferior or sometimes like a fussy little nobody, but the ladies looked up to him as a charming little tyrant who could get things done. Then, too, Mr. Pepys was quick on the draw with his pocketbook when ladies were about. No woman admires a "cheap" man.

CHAPTER 6

Mr. Pepys at the Coronation

THE real charm of Pepys's *Diary* lies in its compilation of little incidents honestly reported by one who seemed to be enjoying himself. Not all the incidents that Mr. Pepys reported were little ones, however. The Coronation, The Plague, the Great Fire would be important in any man's lifetime. A good reporter should supply details of special occasions, and Mr. Pepys did so.

A new King was to be crowned; and the days of April 21-23, 1661, found Mr. Pepys awed by the events of Charles II's coronation. Mr. Pepys began the account with the old worry about the weather, but the sky cleared for the ceremony: the bright sun to a superstitious age must have been a portent of a great and good reign. Dressed in his new velvet coat on the morning of April 22, Mr. Pepys, with the Battens and the Penns, viewed from an upstairs room at Mr. Young's, the flagmaker's, the coronation parade that moved from the Tower to Whitehall. Mr. Pepys sent his wife, meantime, to the Turners in Fleet Street. His own party was provided with wine and good cake, and he stated that it was impossible to relate the glories of the day. He did, however, make the day live again by his inquisitive choice of detail, first of the great parade on the 22nd and then of the actual coronation in Westminster Abbey on the 23rd.

Any reader of Mr. Pepys who has seen a coronation on television must have had the strange feeling that he had witnessed it all before and, indeed, in a manner of speaking, he had; for he had "seen" it in Mr. Pepys's *Diary*. Almost every detail of the parade and of the procession is a gem: General of the Armies George Monk rode bareheaded after the King, and led a spare horse, being Master of the Horse. Mr. Simon Wadlow, the vintner at the "Devil," led a fine company of soldiers, all young comely men, clad in white doublets. There followed the Vice-Chamberlain, Sir George Carteret, leading a company of men dressed like Turks. Upon analysis, the reader realizes that Mr. Pepys's naming names, singling out such specific details, and demonstrating what he himself, the observer, was doing and how the passing show affected him are the factors that make him a great reporter.

Mr. Pepys's station in society was not high enough to merit a seat at the coronation next day, but he got into the chapel at Westminster Abbey just the same. In modern parlance, he crashed the gate. In order to be close to events of this day, he spent the night with Mr. Shepley at the Earl of Sandwich's lodgings at Whitehall. He got up at four in the morning and fell in step with a company that Sir John Denham,[1] Surveyor of the King's Buildings, was leading into the Abbey; and with much ado, Pepys continues, by the favor of Mr. Cooper, Sir John's man, Mr. Pepys made his way up into a great scaffold across the north end of the Abbey, where with a great deal of patience he sat from sometime after four until eleven o'clock before the King came in. He could not see all of the ceremony since his quarters were rather cramped.

With great fidelity, he recounted what he did see, which was considerable: "all the officers of all kinds, so much as the very fiddlers, in red vests. At last comes in the Dean and Prebends of Westminster, with the Bishops (many of them in cloth of gold copes), and after them the Nobility, all in their Parliament robes. . . . Then the Duke, and the King with a scepter (carried by my Lord Sandwich) and sword and mond before him, and the crown too. The King in his robes bare-headed, which was very fine." Mr. Pepys, entranced, listened to the preaching and singing at the coronation and the solemn prayers read from Archbishop Laud's *Book of Common Prayer*. Since he could not see much from his perch, he only heard the great shout go up when the crown was placed on Charles's head. And he saw, or thought he did, the knights put on their caps. Mr. Pepys regretted that, when Lord Cornwallis, Treasurer of His Majesty's Household, flung the silver coronation medals about the Abbey, he could not get hold of a single shining memento of this glittering occasion.

For more than eight hours, including the time taken by the ceremonies, he had occupied his cramped quarters; and Mr. Pepys, always one to give relevant details, recorded that he was under great pressure to relieve himself. Wisely, he crept out of the Abbey before the procession started. He was hungry, too; but quickly making his way within the rails so as to be in a position to see the Royal procession come into the great banquet hall and to manage, somehow, to get a little something from one of the tables, he still took time to notice all that he could, especially his wife sitting in a little stall among the great crowds for whom temporary bleachers had been erected.

The ancient banquet scene entranced him, resembling in many ways, indeed, King Arthur's legendary banquet in the medieval poem *Sir Gawain and the Green Knight*. The Duke of Albemarle was ceremonially eating a bit of the first pretty dish to be set before the King. Despite the regal scene, Mr. Pepys, who was getting hungrier by the minute, went table-hopping outside the rails; he was pleased with the royal feast but was trying to catch a friendly eye. Will Howe,[2] standing at His Lordship's table, mercifully looked his way and, catching Mr. Pepys's signal, whispered to His Lordship who sent four rabbits and a chicken to him. Mr. Michell supplied some bread; and, with Mr. Pepys's strategy as a guide, other beggars, eyeing the proceedings, snatched whatever victuals they could lay their hands on.

The ceremonies over, and so many things to do and see at a wild time like this, any real man would want to be away from the encumbrances of wife and kin. Therefore, Mr. Pepys sent a lame excuse or two to his father's and his own house; he said that he could not come home that night because of the dirt and because a coach could not be had. Stepping into a friend's coffee-house, Harper's, he downed a pot of ale alone. The reports of his movements are none too clear for the rest of the night—nor need they have been, for he was having a wonderful time.

Mrs. Pepys's companion this busy day had been a doctor's wife, a Mrs. Frankleyn, who had attracted Mr. Pepys's roving eye; and the first chance he had, after he had had something to eat from His Lordship's table, he climbed up into the scaffold to kiss the pretty lady. By and by, he had taken the ladies down to Mr. Bowyer's lodgings and, finally, to the Hunts', offering his wife's pretty companion the privilege of sleeping with Mrs. Pepys that night, while he went out into the streets crowded with gallants and bullyboys and their women who stopped him at every turn to force him to drink the King's health while they knelt on faggots. This night would be a dangerous one for any Puritan man to be abroad, but Pepys drank willingly, and his head was clear enough for him to wonder how the ladies did tipple. His head, or at least his account of what followed, clears.

He reports that Mr. Thornbury, yeoman to the King's wine cellar, dispensed free drinks to the ladies and gallant sparks, and they drank the King's health steadily until one of the men fell down stark drunk and vomited mightily. With unsteady steps, enough being enough, Mr. Pepys sought bed with Mr. Shepley at His Lordship's lodgings; but no sooner was he abed, he recalls, than his head began to hum and he too vomited; and, if ever he was "foxed," it was then. He fell asleep betimes, and woke next morning in a wet bed.

Thus did the day end with joy everywhere, but with a minor accident or two: Sergeant Glynne, a Puritan, had had the misfortune of being crushed to death when his horse fell on him, and a woman had had an eye put out by a boy's flinging a firebrand into her coach. The wonder of life and the sheer joy of living it and reporting it are the very heart of Mr. Pepys's *Diary*.

CHAPTER 7

Schoolman and Bibliophile

I *Cambridge*

THE best way to be reminded of one's early schooling is to meet an old schoolmate. On March 15, 1660, while Mr. Pepys was piling his utensils and other belongings on a hired cart to move to His Lordship's dwelling, preparatory to going with him to Holland, he met Tom Alcock, "one that went to school with me at Huntingdon but I had not seen him these sixteen years." Samuel Pepys went later to St. Paul's school in London and then entered sizar at Trinity Hall, Cambridge; but he transferred to Magdalene College, from which he graduated as a bachelor of arts in 1653. His college career was normal; he got a scholarship, was reprimanded for being drunk, and retained a typical alumni sentimentality for his college. He did something really fine for Magdalene, however, for he gave her his books, now affectionately cared for in the Pepysian Library at Magdalene College.

In the *Diary* Mr. Pepys expressed his affection for the schools that he attended. He liked to visit the old scenes and, indeed, carried on a love affair with his schools, especially Magdalene. He was the best type of educated man imaginable, for not only had he learned much at Cambridge, but he also increased his knowledge daily. And Mr. Pepys was a typical seventeenth-century man in the sense that he liked to display his Classical learning, especially in the languages, living and dead. At the theater, at home, at the office, or to hide, as it were, his presence in some unconscionable place, a Latin or French, Greek or Italian phrase would come to his mind and he would write it down in the *Diary*.

When he took his younger brother John to Cambridge on February 25, 1660, entering him at Christ's College, Mr. Pepys and Father Pepys visited about the ancient grounds and buildings, drank hard at the local inns, had a good dinner that was paid for by "a club"—by the "chipping in" of several old schoolmates. After the customary Saturday night disputation was over, Mr. Pepys observed that "there was nothing at all left of the old preciseness in their discourse."

Mr. Pepys received an honorary master of arts degree from Magdalene College in June, 1660, and finished paying for it on August 14, 1660. Always the master at recording significant details, Mr. Pepys reported: "My father, after dinner, takes leave, after I had given him 40s. for the last half year for my brother John at Cambridge. I did also make even with Mr. Fairbrother for my degree of Master of Arts, which cost me about £9 16s."[1]

Loyal alumnus Samuel Pepys visited Cambridge often, especially when he could combine a visit with one to his home at Brampton: "Up by three o'clock this morning and rode to Cambridge," he reported on July 15, 1661. Arriving there, he went first to the barber's, then to Christ's College, "and found my brother John at eight o'clock in bed, which vexed me," he complained. He spent a good day, nevertheless, meeting Dr. Fairbrother whom he treated to drinks at "The Rose," and he sent for Mr. Sanchy of Magdalene and other old schoolmates, treated them too, and they were "very merry," he admitted in a favorite phrase.

On a later visit to Cambridge, on October 10, 1662, the schoolman participated in activities more weighty than drinking wine; for he was provided with cap, gown, and hood, and invited to help elect officers of the university. Mr. Pepys was "much pleased of doing this jobb of work" which he had long wished to do, for he always enjoyed the brave glory and swishing silks of an academic procession. On the same visit (October 15), he took pride in showing King's College Chapel, Trinity College, and St. John's College library to a friend, Mr. Cooke.

II *From Cambridge to Brampton*

Scholar, linguist, antiquarian, and loyal alumnus, Mr. Pepys enjoyed a leisurely visit to Cambridge and his Brampton home. On his way on October 7, 1667, by coach with Mrs. Pepys and Deb in fine style, and Messrs. Hewer and Murford following on horseback, Mr. Pepys's party stopped at Mrs. Aynsworth's inn, the "Reindeer," famous among the country fellows and wayfarers for good, rough sport. Mr. Pepys admitted to himself that he had known Mrs. Aynsworth "better than they think for" when

she had kept an inn at Cambridge before the university authorities ran her away from there because of vile reputation, but her
reputation and her salty comrades had followed her to the "Reindeer." He recalled that she had taught him a very lewd song
entitled "Full Forty Times Over," but with Mrs. Pepys and the
new maid along, he could not very well re-create the old ac-
quaintanceship with Mrs. Aynsworth. Mr. Pepys's party drove
on to Cambridge, and they stopped at the "Rose," for Mr. Pepys
wanted to look at Dorothy Drawwater, the vintner's daughter
there, who had been mentioned by His Grace of Newcastle in
the play *Sir Martin Marall* that Mr. Pepys knew so well.

Come home to his *Alma Mater,* Mr. Pepys regaled himself as
any alumnus does when he returns home. He visited the buildings, showed the ladies Trinity College, St. John's Library, and
the inside of King's College Chapel. He was delighted with his
females in their pretty morning gowns, and proud to find himself
in the condition to show them off. He walked importantly about
the town, talking to the drawers concerning town matters; but
he was really wanting to see how many denizens would recognize
little Sam Pepys who once had been a student here; and he was
hoping that some would know that he had turned to be "a big
wheel" in London city.

Arriving at Brampton, he was pleased with the sight of the
cottage and with how well his father had kept it. A quick minute's survey, and his busy imagination showed that, with a reasonable outlay of money, the place could become a good country
seat. There can be no doubt that Mr. Pepys envisioned himself as
Sir Samuel Pepys at his seat at Brampton.

After dinner, he walked to Hinchingbroke, the country seat
of the numerous clan of that name. Mr. Pepys enjoyed the temporary role of distinguished visitor, Lady Hinchingbroke pumped
him dry of every drop of news of the city, and they spent practically the entire afternoon walking about the grounds, pausing
to rest, and conversing. Her attention flattered him, and he has
rewarded her in the *Diary* with a tribute to her gentility. No
conversation with members of the Hinchingbroke-Montagu-Crew-
Carteret clan could last long without reference to money; for,
generally, they were impecunious members of the minor nobility,
living always on the knife-edge of financial embarrassment. Mr.
Pepys reported in the *Diary* the evidence of Lady Hinchingbroke's financial plight: Her Ladyship had sold close to nine

hundred pounds of the family plate and was now seeking a buyer for a section of her best draperies. Mr. Pepys thought to himself that he would be willing, almost, to buy a piece or two if the suit could be broken.

The main business of the next two days, October 10 and 11, was retrieving and checking the money that Mr. Pepys had sent to Brampton for burying in mid-June. He was so cautious in this activity that not even to the *Diary* had he whispered until now the purpose of his mission. He did not, however, make a beeline to the hiding place; he had spent the morning of October 10 talking with his father about Paulina Pepys and her spinster-hood.

III *Scientist*

Schoolman Pepys's catholicity of interests cannot be too much emphasized. Painstaking office-holder, bibliophile, historian, antiquarian, musician, news reporter, columnist, critic, and what not, he was also a scientist at heart. The term "experimental science" would nearly assess his interest in science and in mechanics. He was interested in finding out how a thing worked, or could be made to work, or a better way of doing something. On February 27, 1663, he attended an impressive lecture on kidneys and ureters by Dr. Christopher Terne at Chyrurgeon's Hall. After the lecture, Mr. Pepys joined the learned company at dinner, and drank the King's health from a gilt cup (given to the company long ago by Henry VIII) with bells hanging on it, which every man rang, according to custom, by shaking after he had drunk the full draught. After dinner, the company went to the demonstration room where Dr. Charles Scarborough exhibited a cadaver, the remains of a lusty seaman, hanged for robbery.

With his precious gift of furnishing details, Mr. Pepys reported that he had touched the cadaver with his bare hand and that it had felt cold. He learned, among other scientific curiosities, how effective a silken noose was in contrast to a stiff one; the doctor explained that the victim, hanged with a silk noose, felt no pain, since circulation of the blood ceased in an instant. On a tour of the store room, Mr. Pepys inspected the bodies and was instructed in physiology and pathology of the kidneys and ureters. He inquired about the ways of gallstones and was carefully instructed; he must have been personally interested, since he had been operated on for gallstones and often had trouble with water. He attended the afternoon lectures concerning the heart, lungs, and other vital organs, to his great pleasure and satisfaction. Mr. Pepys was a thoroughly well-informed and sophisticated man-of-the-world.

His reputation as a man who could get things done, especially at the navy office; his presence, always, at the regular Monday meetings called by the Lord High Admiral of the Fleet, James, Duke of York; his knack of getting himself appointed to things; his known interest in the sciences; and the fact that he helped Mr. Thomas Povy, the Treasurer of Tangier, unsnarl his knotted accounts induced Mr. Povy to propose Pepys for membership in the Royal Society, a regular collegium of scientific virtuosos. Mr. Pepys would be at home in such sophisticated learned company, and on February 15, 1665, he was admitted.[2] Mr. Pepys had just come from dinner with the amiable old sokers of Trinity House, an ancient maritime organization in which he held membership,[3] and he was unanimously approved by the members present who included Lord Brouncker, Sirs Philip Neale, Robert Moray, Thomas Harvey, and Drs. Boyle, Hooke, Goddard, Clarke, and Whistler.

IV *Linguist and Bibliophile*

A fact about Mr. Pepys not generally recalled is his versatility as a scholar. He had a good working knowledge of several languages: Latin, Greek, French, Spanish, and a little Italian. He actually put these languages to use in the *Diary*, albeit sometimes only, as has been observed, to conceal a peccadillo. He spoke French, as did Mrs. Pepys, read books written in Latin, and had an ear that could detect faulty accentuation. The respect that seventeenth-century man held for Classical learning and for proficiency in foreign tongues was shared by Mr. Pepys. It was still the practice for the young scholars in the public schools and in the universities to contend in Latin and to compose in foreign tongues. Latin, in particular, and Greek, to a lesser extent, maintained a stubborn foothold in places where they had been honored in practice and usage in the courts, in the church, and in the schools. Allowing for the fact that Mr. Pepys's own Latin and Greek from the Cambridge days might have been getting a little rusty, it must be recognized that he was a seventeenth-century man, living at a time when the mighty examples of Athenian genius were cultivated with daily and nightly devotion and Greek and Latin were read and written and even spoken by the average respectable English schoolboy.

The reference in the *Diary* is brief but significant where Mr. Pepys recorded that on May 31, 1660, he had begun to instruct young Edward Montagu, His Lordship's son in Latin; and Pepys knew enough Latin to note that the boy had had a good foundation in it. He also examined Lady Sandwich's page Laud Crisp on December 7 and was pleased that he was so far advanced in the subject. When Mr. Pepys visited Lady Jemimah Sandwich at the family seat at Hinchingbroke on October 10, 1667, she had sent to the local boarding school run by Headmaster Taylor to fetch His Lordship's twins to greet Mr. Pepys, who could not miss the opportunity to take them into the summer house to examine them in their schooling. And lest there be any doubt about Mr. Pepys's knowledge, one may read his account of his testing the little fellows: "and do find them so well endowed in their learning that I was amazed at it: they repeating a whole ode without book out of Horace, and did give me a very good account of any thing almost, and did make me readily very good Latin, and did give me good account of their Greek grammar . . . ; and so grave and manly as I never saw, I confess, nor could have believed; so that they will be fit to go to Cambridge in two years at most. . . ."

There is no doubt that Mr. Pepys could translate Latin. Although Mr. Pepys's brother John was not an impressive scholar at Cambridge, he gave Mr. Pepys still another chance to put his own knowledge of Latin to work. On February 21, 1666, Mr. Pepys recorded that John had written a Latin letter to him from Cambridge, stating that he was soon to have a Master of Arts degree and would be going into holy orders at Lent.

Contact with books, with scholars, and with language-at-work always struck a happy response in Mr. Pepys; and the day of February 4, 1663, despite a temporary adversity, cheered him for the days to come. He had gone to St. Paul's school for Apposition Day; and, being an alumnus, as he listened to the speeches, he found them much as they had been when he was a student; they dealt with the seven liberal sciences. Leaving St. Paul's, for the nonce, Mr. Pepys went to the Court of Arches where a judge was sitting with his proctors, dressed in their habits, who pleaded in Latin. As soon as the proceedings permitted, Pepys returned to the congenial atmosphere of St. Paul's

to see the head forms examined in Latin, Greek, and Hebrew;
but he thought that the scholars did not answer so well as they
had in his time, except for geography.

Old Boy Samuel Pepys was honored when Dr. Crumlum presented him to many persons as the donor of Stephanus in four
volumes (and Mr. Pepys said to himself, "cost me £4.10s"). At
his request, Dr. Crumlum showed Mr. Pepys an old edition of
Dean Colet's famous English grammar, and Pepys turned with
pleasure to Colet's epistle to the children, particularly to see the
unique phrasing of the Apostles' Creed "borne of the cleane
Virgin Mary." Such stimulating intellectual fare diverted him,
and he invited Mr. Elborough, the only old schoolmate that he
could find, to a cook's shop to dinner; but Mr. Pepys found him
a fool as he ever was or worse, he complained, perhaps with
crusty delight.

One of Mr. Pepys's favorite writers was Sir Francis Bacon,
who had written many of his weighty scientific and philosophical
works in Latin because he had decided that the English language
lacked the dignity and precision to express his thoughts. Mr.
Pepys, also a seventeenth-century man, so delighted in Bacon's
inductive philosophical processes that he asked John Pepys to
put his Latin to practice in translating a section of Bacon's *De
Augmentis Scientiarum*. On October 29, 1666, Mr. Pepys expressed great displeasure with brother John's translation; and he
knew enough Latin, himself, to report that John had done it
"meanely," meaning literally, "and with no life at all."

Antiquarian, preacher, humorist, scholar, and Mr. Pepys's
friend, Dr. Thomas Fuller provided him not only with some great
and favorite books that he had written, *The Church History of
Britain*, *The Worthies of England*, and others, but also with
good advice in the practice of speaking Latin (January 22, 1661):
"The best way to begin a sentence if a man should be out and
forget his last sentence . . . is to begin with an Utcunque." There
were many times, however, when Mr. Pepys would employ his
generous and versatile knowledge of languages in situations far
less worthy than scholarship; but, after all, he actually put the
languages to work.

V *Favorite Books*

A scholar should take frequent inventory of his books and
papers and do what Mr. Pepys did at year's end, 1664: keep the

treasures and "tear what is either boyish or not to be worth keeping." Among the quaint items that Mr. Pepys retained was a Latin charm: *Sanguis mane in te, Sicut Christus fuit in se. . . .*

Mr. Pepys maintained a bibliophile's interest in books. In his daily walks about the streets of London, book collecting took a good deal of his time. If ever there was a genuine bibliophile, it was Mr. Pepys. He loved to fondle their splendid leather bindings, to test their paper or vellum leaves and run his fingers along the edges, to try the leather and the buckram backs, and to test the clasps to find out if they fastened securely. Even when he wasn't sure of the material or intellectual value of a book, he would look at it in the bookseller's stall, think about it for a day or two, and then, maybe reluctantly, he would purchase it, or buy the gatherings and arrange for a skilled craftsman to cut the pages and bind and cover them to suit him. The result of his long love affair with books is the Pepysian Library at Magdalene College, Cambridge. A young man, he could hardly have been giving serious thought to such a memorial of his name.

A dutiful reader, he was always busy and inquisitive among the pages; but he was not a profound scholar. Seventeenth-century man was a reading man, and Mr. Pepys was typical of his time. If a book were being talked about, he wanted to get it, especially if it contained curiosities and recondite information. Quite aside from what the modern reader might call "literary value," Mr. Pepys valued antiquarian bits and oddments. Although he was no Democritus Junior, he had Robert Burton's love of curiosities; but, unlike Burton, Pepys sought for curios outside of books as well as inside. For certain, a partial explanation of his love of books was the desire to own things. Mr. Pepys was really a collector of plate, paintings, furniture, clothes. On November 14, 1660, as a single instance, he bought at St. Paul's Churchyard a Latin comedy entitled *Cornelianum Dolium.*

A real lover of books, a reading man, and a scholar in the best sense of this overworked term, Mr. Pepys kept contact with what scientists, historians, theologians, playwrights, and poets were doing. He bought their books; he read them; he loved them, and gave them a permanent home in his house. If a book was being much cried up, as Mr. Pepys might say, he would want to read it and to own it; for he would not wish to admit in company that he had not read a current best-seller. A single illustration of one of his procedures in buying a book must suffice. He reported, on

December 26, 1662: "Hither come Mr. Battersby; and we falling into a discourse of a new book of drollery in verse called Hudebras, I would needs go find it out, and met with it at the Temple: cost 2s.6d." When Mr. Pepys read Samuel Butler's rough lampoon of the quixotic Puritan knight he thought the satire "so silly an abuse" that he was ashamed of it. Later that day, meeting him at dinner, he sold the book to Mr. Townsend for eighteen pence, losing a shilling in the transaction.

The long anti-Puritan poem *Hudibras* was so famous in its day that Mr. Pepys eventually bought a copy for his library and provided, moreover, a good account of his feeling for books. On December 10, 1663, he recorded: "I could not tell whether to lay out my money for books of pleasure, as plays, which my nature was most earnest in, but at last after seeing Chaucer, Dugdale's History of Paul's, Stow's London, Gesner, History of Trent, besides Shakespeare, Jonson, and Beaumont's plays, I at last chose Dr. Fuller's Worthys, The Cabbala or Collection of Letters of State, and a little book, Delices de Hollande, with another little book or two, all of good use or serious pleasure: and Hudibras both parts, the book now in greatest fashion for drollery. . . ." He eventually bought them all; and, for good use or serious pleasure, Mr. Pepys, scholar, purchased, read, and bequeathed many books.

CHAPTER 8

Mr. Pepys As Musician

MUSIC had an important place in an average Pepys day. On Sunday, December 9, 1660, he went to Whitehall to see the Duke of York; and, after this visit, Mr. Pepys reports that he went to chapel and sat in Mr. Blagrave's pew, "and there did sing my part with another before the King and with much ease." It is difficult to ascertain what part Mr. Pepys sang. A guess would be tenor or baritone, for he was of slight build. The fact that he marveled at a little man's singing bass is also suggestive of the quality of his own voice. On a rather typical Pepys's Sunday (September 15, 1667) the Reverend Daniel Mills, Pepys's rector at St. Olave's, and Mrs. Mills had come to dinner, as well as three gentlemen by appointment to sing with Pepys: Messrs. Pelling, Wallington, and Piggott. In his usual accurate way, Mr. Pepys reports that "Wallington being a very little fellow, did sing a most excellent bass. Here we sung several good things. . . ." He adds a professional-sounding opinion: "I am more and more confirmed that singing with many voices is not singing but a sort of instrumental musique; the sense of the words being lost by not being heard, and especially as they set them with fugues of words, one after another, whereas singing properly, I think, should be put with one or two voices at most and the counterpoint."

Mr. Pepys thought well enough of his own singing to employ a voice instructor. On June 25, 1661, he paid a deposit of twenty shillings to Theodore Goodgroome and agreed to pay him twenty shillings a month "to teach me to sing." "And so we began, and I hope to have come to something in it," he added. The first song that he attempted was entitled "Cruda la bella." Undoubtedly, Mr. Pepys kept his voice active by singing for his own personal delight: "At night to my chamber to read and sing. . . ." The entry for Good Friday, March 28, 1662, is common enough in the *Diary*; for Mr. Pepys was the kind of singer who sang whenever he thought someone was listening: in "house of office," at his desk, in a coach, or walking. And, like Chaucer's summoner, Pepys would "bear a stiff burden" to any other singing person by supplying a counterpoint to an air that another sang. He also wrote music for words, and tried to sing the song in the patient hearing of any friend who would listen.

I *Mary Mercer, Maid and Musician*

A beloved companion in singing, and other activities, was Mary Mercer who came to the Pepys household on September 9, 1664, as a companion and servant to Mrs. Pepys. Any new turn of events, however slight, would bring laughter to merry Samuel Pepys and put him in such good humor that he would resolve to brighten the pattern of days already bright: "and so back again home, and there my wife and Mercer and Tom and I sat till eleven at night, singing and fiddling, and a great joy it is to see me master of so much pleasure in my house, that it is and will be still, I hope, a constant pleasure to me to be at home." He was quite excited to discover such musical skills right there in his household: Mary played pretty well upon the harpsicon and, if only ordinary tunes, she had a good musical hand. She "sings a little," adds Mr. Pepys, "but hath a good voyce and eare. My boy, a brave boy, sings finely, and is the most pleasant boy at present." Musical Mary Mercer was a girl to please his very heart. When he found her playing on the viol at home on September 28, he called the instrument "pretty," probably meaning its music; and he reports his musical accompaniment: "and so I to the Vyall and singing till late, and so to bed."

It is never quite possible to separate Mr. Pepys's activities into categories. He lived life in the round and a Pepys's day was a flavorsome congeries of occurrences, big and little, and music often provided the flavor. On July 30, 1666, Mr. Pepys reports: "Thence home; and to sing with my wife and Mercer in the garden; and coming in I find my wife plainly dissatisfied with me, that I can spend so much time with Mercer, teaching her to sing, and could never take the pains with her. Which I acknowledge; but it is because that the girl do take musique mighty readily, and she do not, and musique is the thing of the world that I love most, and all the pleasure almost that I can now take." If it was the pleasure almost, it was not all. And it was no wonder that

Mrs. Pepys felt a jealous twinge, for Mr. Pepys was currently mixing other pleasures with his music. On the night of June 19, 1666, he had sung a little in the garden with Mrs. Pepys and Mary Mercer and of the latter he confessed, "I feel myself begin to love too much by handling of her breasts in a' morning when she dresses me, they being the finest that ever I saw in my life, that is the truth of it." Four days later when Mr. Pepys got wind of a bitter wrangling that his wife had had with Mercer and learned that the girl would quit the household that very day, he confessed going to his room and that he would have cried had not people pressed business upon him.

II *Mr. Pepys's Musical Companions*

Not only with Mary Mercer in his house and elsewhere did Mr. Pepys associate but also with other versatile musical persons farther removed. Music, if no more than a snatch of song, was part of his day's activities. On December 8, 1665, though The Plague was still raging, Mr. Pepys had company at his household at Greenwich, including Mrs. Knepp, the actress, and her husband, "a melancholy, jealous-looking fellow"; Dr. and Mrs. Pierce;[1] Captain Rolt; Mr. and Mrs. Edward Coleman;[2] and Mr. Pepys's good singing friend and music-lover Mr. Thomas Hill, the merchant. Always favoring the reader of the *Diary* with an exquisite blend of incident, Mr. Pepys reports that the group had "most excellent musique in abundance, and a good supper, dancing." Then he adds flavor to the report: "and a pleasant scene of Mrs. Knipp's [*sic*] rising sicke from the table, but whispered me it was for some hard word or other her husband gave her just now when she laughed and was more merry than ordinary. But we got her in humour again, and mighty merry; . . ." Not even the presence of a surly, jealous husband could squelch the group's high spirits. They sang and danced until two in the morning "with most complete content," reports Mr. Pepys in a singing phrase. Mr. Hill, who stayed the night with the Pepyses, listened appreciatively next day to Mr. Pepys's composition of a song "Beauty retire." And the honest, accurate Diarist reports: "which he likes, only excepts against two notes in the base, but likes the whole very well."

The singing mood prevailed next day, December 10; for Mr. Hill, still a guest, and Pepys went to visit another singing friend,

Captain George Cocke, "for some newes." The Captain prevailed on Pepys to stay for dinner; and, dutifully, he sent for Mrs. Pepys. Sir Edmund Pooly and Mr. Pepys's good friend and fellow diarist, John Evelyn,[3] stopped by; "and there we sang some things." But one of the guests who had to leave precipitately broke the enchanted evening. There never is a trite situation in the *Diary*, for Mr. Pepys reports the reason for Mr. Andrews' haste to leave the group: "his wife looking every hour to be brought to bed." No decent husband, after all, should be raising his voice in song with his wife about to give birth. "He gone, Mr. Hill and I continued our musique, one thing after another, late till supper, and so to bed with great pleasure."

III *Pepys Works at Music Composition*

Practically the same group as of December 10 visited at Mr. Pepys's bidding during the holidays (January 3, 1666). Although "Knipp and her surly husband" were among the guests, Mr. Pepys prevailed on Mr. Coleman to sing his composition "Beauty retire"; and Mr. Pepys praised his own song and his guests added commendation. "Then to dancing and supper, and mighty merry till Mr. Rolt come in, whose pain of the toothache made him no company, and spoilt ours," Mr. Pepys reports, adding that Mrs. Pepys's teeth, too, "fell to akeing," and the company broke up but "all with a good song." He praised his song again (February 22), and he rewards the reader of the *Diary* with a splendid description of Mrs. Knepp who sang it for him: "I spent all the night talking with this baggage and teaching her my song of 'Beauty retire' which she sings and makes go most rarely, and a very fine song it seems to be." Always a master of the apt phrase, Mr. Pepys indicates how important the singer is to make the song successful. Praise from the listener as well as the singer, albeit indirect praise, came to Mr. Pepys on August 22, 1666. Mrs. Knepp told him that the song was being "mightily cried up"; he felt quite proud of his growing reputation as a composer, and announced another song "It is decreed." A better one, he thought, although it was still unfinished.

Enjoying Dr. and Mrs. Pierce's hospitality on November 9, 1666, Mr. Pepys seemed to have had a captive audience, for he reports that, "after some trifling discourse" and a "first bout of dancing," he and Mrs. Knepp sang. Captain Downing had politely insisted on hearing "Beauty retire" which Mrs. Knepp had "spread abroad." Inching its way upward in popularity, Mr. Pepys's song drew his own praise and also the Captain's: "and he extols it above anything he ever heard, and, without flattery, I know it is good in its kind."

When the airs sang themselves in Mr. Pepys's head, he sought advice from professional musicians. Mr. John Berkenshaw tutored Pepys in the intricacies of notes and grace notes and in ways to make a tune come right, and they met in many spirited sessions. By February 27, 1662, Mr. Pepys had so mastered composition that he told Berkenshaw that his system was "somewhat lame." The professor took offense, and he and Pepys "fell to angry words, so that in a pet he flung out" of the house. Mr. Pepys, who records that he had planned to dismiss his instructor in any case, adds that he thought he had learned all that Berkenshaw could teach him.

Making use of Mr. Berkenshaw's instructions from time to time, Samuel Pepys composed the tune for one of Ben Jonson's songs. The stateliness of the first two lines suggests *fortissimo*: "It is decreed nor shall thy fate, O Rome! Resist my vow, though hills were set on hills." On April 5, 1666, he put notes to the song; and he then polished and burnished his composition as the spirit moved him. "In all my ridings in the coach and intervals my mind hath been full these three weeks of setting in music 'It is Decreed,'" he reported on April 18. The tune concerned him constantly, the notes running through the mazes of his mind, and he would go home and tinker and tamper with the elusive score as he did on July 27. By August 22, when he met Mrs. Knepp at the Exchequer and the actress praised "Beauty retire," saying that it was being "mightily cried up," Mr. Pepys confided to himself that he had achieved a better composition in "It is Decreed" but that he still had not finished it. After church on November 11, he claimed to have finished "putting time" to the song.

It would be amusing to digress to follow Mr. Pepys in and out of Mrs. Knepp's lodgings on November 14, Mr. Knepp standing by, and to record the myriad things he did that day before and after. But on that day he wished to have Mrs. Knepp sing "It is Decreed." By now "It is Decreed" needed a better name than "song" and better language to report its première. "After dinner I to teach her my new recitative of 'It is Decreed,' of which she learnt a good part, and I do well like it and believe shall be well

SAMUEL PEPYS

pleased when she hath it all, and that it will be found an agreeable thing." Mr. Pepys had fitted the tune to the theme and the
temper of Ben Jonson's lines, and the reader can readily imagine
Mrs. Knepp's striking a pose to sing the declamatory song.

The music needed more body, nevertheless; and Mr. Pepys began to set a bass to the song late on the night of December 10,
but he needed professional help. Over drinks, no doubt, at the
"Dog," on December 19, he got Mr. John Hingston, the composer and organist, to help him set in the bass notes. Mr. Pepys's
accuracy in reporting details is in evidence and he captures, as
well, the nuance of faint praise expressed by the professional to
the amateur musician: "and I took him to the Dog Taverne and
got him to set me a bass to my 'It is Decreed' which I think will
go well, but he commends the song not knowing the words, but
says the ayre is good, and believes the words are plainly expressed. He is of my mind against having the 8ths unnecessarily
in composition. This did all please me mightily." The fact of the
matter was that amateur musician Pepys could not manage the
intricacies of quavers and semi-quavers, and Mr. Hingston probably advised him to forego their overuse.

Mr. Hingston's bass fitted well, and on Christmas Day Mr.
Pepys risked teaching his wife and her maid the song, and the
result pleased him mightily. But better voices were needed for
the song, and on January 28, 1667, Mary Mercer was called in to
practice and perfect it. There can be little doubt that Mr. Pepys
and Miss Mercer hummed the tune throughout a busy year; but
they sang it in earnest on January 9, 1668, after one of Mr. Pepys's
active days at the theater. He appeared still to be not quite satisfied with the song, however, and he had a mind to have her learn
to sing it, "and she will do it well," he mused. The next day he
took Miss Mercer home "to teach her more of 'It is Decreed'"
and to sing a repertory of songs.

A male voice would be better for "It is Decreed," thought Mr.
Pepys; and he decided, after "pricking out" the song on March
24, that he would give it to his friend Henry Harris, the actor, to
sing; but this occasion did not mark the perfecting of Mr. Pepys's
musical effort. Standing at Pepys's elbow as he manipulated the
notes, listening as he hummed the musical parts and fitted them
into the score, and watching him as he waited for others' approval as they, in turn, sang "It is Decreed," the reader of the
Diary learns the ways of an amateur composer.

IV   *Mr. Pepys Practices on Strings*

Stringed instruments have a way of getting out of tune, of gathering dust in corners, of losing steel and catgut strings, and of finding their way into pawnshops. Mr. Pepys kept his musical instruments in good repair; he practiced on them diligently; he took music lessons, and, if he pawned an instrument in an earlier time when his fortunes were low, he retrieved it: "called at Mr. Blagrave's, where I took up my note that he had of mine for 40s., which he two years ago did give me as a pawn while he had my lute" (March 18, 1660). Pepys lent the instrument to His Lordship; and, after they had both returned from Holland, Mr. Pepys retrieved it on August 10.

On the 25th he secured a book of lute lessons in the most charming way imaginable: Judge Fowler's son, the apothecary, brought his father's music book that His Honour had left at the drug store for Mr. Pepys, the book from which "he formerly did use to play when a young man and had the use of his hand." Instrument and lessons handy and plucking the strings betimes, Mr. Pepys got a music lesson on November 9. He got it in the usual charming Pepysian way, for the lesson was given gratis by Mr. Lewis Evans, the musician, when he and Pepys were waiting in Sir Harry Wright's pantry while His Lordship was upstairs looking at hole cards.

Whether diligent practice damaged Mr. Pepys's lute would be hard to discover, but it found its way into the instrument maker's hand for repairs. Mr. Pepys retrieved it on October 25, 1661, and he supplies precise information concerning its new neck and double strings. The instrument-maker, Mr. Hunt, sent a teacher, Mr. Hill, on November 7 to instruct Pepys in the theorbo, a double-necked bass lute, but Mr. Pepys states that he did not like the instructor's playing or singing and that he politely sent him away. On December 7, footman of His Lordship, Emmanuel Luffe, played excellently on Mr. Pepys's theorbo and brought forth such music that Mr. Pepys discovered the splendor of the instrument.

There is evidence in the *Diary* that Mr. Pepys took lessons, practiced sedulously, received advice concerning his theorbo and viol, mended and refurbished them throughout the years, and ordered new ones made. On July 30, 1666, moreover, he hired a lute-master to give theorbo lessons to his servant boy; and Mr.

Pepys constantly tried to cultivate music in other servants and in Mrs. Pepys. On October 22, the young servant had made such progress that Mr. Pepys was pleased mightily when, upon returning home, he found the lad playing a duet with Mr. William Caesar, lute-master and composer. As for Mr. Pepys, he had acquired such musical competence on strings that he could take his part with professional musicians. After providing dinner on November 15, 1667, Pepys sat with Messrs. Caesar, Blagrave, and boastful little Pelham Humphreys—musicians all; and Pepys states in the *Diary* that Humphreys played the theorbo; Mr. Caesar, the French lute; and he, Mr. Pepys, the viol. "But made mean musique," he complained; he was disgusted to the point of profanity with mincing Mr. Humphreys' boasting.

Always at ease in the company of musicians, cultivating their friendship and seeking their professional advice, Mr. Pepys introduces them frequently in the *Diary*. After church on March 29, 1668, he is stirred to make a resolution for the future. He had invited Henry Harris, the actor, and John Bannister, composer, to dinner, "most extraordinary company both, the latter for musique of all sorts, the former for everything: here we sang, and Bannister played on the theorbo, and afterwards Bannister played on his flageolet, and I had very good discourse with him about musique so confirming some of my new notions about musique that it puts me upon a resolution to go on and make a scheme and theory of musique not yet ever made in the world."

Despite this proud resolution, Mr. Pepys remained an amateur musician; but he was a devoted, determined, and versatile amateur who wrote songs and who sedulously applied lip and fingers to woodwinds and strings, respectively. When Mrs. Knepp sang Davenant's song "The Lark" at a supper on September 4, 1668, Mr. Pepys was inspired to write a bass for it a few nights later; but a sharp argument that day at the navy office had left him in a melancholy mood and he was not pleased with his musical efforts.

Of his compositions, "Beauty retire" was, really, Pepys's favorite song. He took the lyric from Davenant's play *The Siege of Rhodes*. In the Pepys portrait by John Hales at The National Portrait Gallery, "Beauty retire" is the song that the painting reveals in Mr. Pepys's hand. Two other songs composed during the time of the *Diary* and mentioned frequently in it are "It is Decreed" and "Gaze Not on Swans." "Gaze Not on Swans" is not certainly identified as Pepys's composition, for there is a song to the same words by Henry Lawes.

As for Mr. Pepys's playing, he played well or practiced on the treble viol, the lyra viol, the bass viol, the lute, and the theorbo. And on June 5, 1660, Pepys mentioned a musical session with His Lordship who borrowed a lieutenant's cither; but Pepys does not state clearly who applied the plectrum to its wire strings. When he heard a Frenchman play the guitar "most extreme well" on July 27, 1661, Mr. Pepys dismissed the instrument as a bauble; and, although it was His Lordship's favorite instrument (*Diary*, November 17, 1665), Mr. Pepys was troubled that Signor Francisco's great musical talents and such pains "should have been taken upon so bad an instrument" as the guitar (August 5, 1667).

V *Proficiency with Woodwinds*

Mr. Pepys appears to have preferred wind instruments to others. The flageolet was his favorite, and he carried one about in his pocket, just as he often did a book of plays or any little handy object. To pass the time with music, Mr. Pepys would play the flageolet anywhere—in a boat, in the coach, in his garden, while accompanying his wife's uncertain singing, or between drinks and waiting for a dish of poached eggs at a refectory near Temple Bar on February 9, 1660. "I took out my flageolette and piped," May 14, 1660, is a typical description of merry Mr. Pepys's attitude and musical activity. He tried to improve his skill, nevertheless, by taking lessons from Master Thomas Greeting.

On January 16, 1660, at a musical session of varied accomplishments at the "Green Dragon" on Lambeth Hill, the two Messrs. Pinkney and Messrs. Smith, Harrison, Morrice, Shepley, and Pepys sang "all sorts of things." He adds that he ventured many things at first sight and afterward played on his flageolet and remained absorbed in musical activities until the night was far spent, and his going home late gave him still another opportunity to add charming musical detail to the *Diary*: "I staid up till the bell-man came by with his bell just under my window as I was writing of this very line, and cried, 'Past one of the clock, and a cold, frosty, windy morning.'"

The flageolet itself could stand improvement, Pepys thought; and in the middle of a busy morning on January 20, 1668, while on the way to and from the Exchequer, he stopped at Mr. Drumbleby's, the flageolet maker's, "to advise about the making of a flageolet to go low and soft." As usual supplying the relevant detail, Mr. Pepys continues: "and he do shew me a way which do do, and also a fashion of having two pipes of the same note fastened together, so as I can play on one, and then echo it upon the other, which is mighty pretty." When Mr. Drumbleby delivered the new instrument, its tones were so dulcet that Mr. Pepys was pleased mightily.

When he attempted to learn to play a reed instrument, however, Mr. Pepys encountered difficulty to the point of resolving "to show the world a simpler way" to master its intricacies: "So home to my chamber" he enters in the *Diary*, April 8, 1668, "to be fingering of my Recorder, and getting of the scale of musique without book, which I at last see is necessary for a man that would understand musique, as it is now taught to be understood, though it be a ridiculous and troublesome way. . . ." He appears to have made no progress with the recorder since he mentions his encounter with the instrument tersely in conjunction with a purchase of Mr. Greeting's book of flageolet lessons for a shilling on April 16, 1668: "begun this day to learn the Recorder."

VI *At the Harpsichord*

His accomplishments on the harpsichord could have been only modest at best. On February 22, 1661, Mr. Pepys had gone to see Theophila Turner's new harpsichord that was being made in Bishopsgate Street, but it was not ready and he did not see it. After church, "where a stranger preached like a fool" on March 31, 1661, Mr. Pepys stepped in to try to "woo" Mrs. Turner to give him a lesson on the new harpsichord, and he reports his anger at her refusal. Mr. Pepys decided, eventually, to buy his own harpsichord and went looking for the maker who had lived in Bishopgate Street before the Great Fire. He did not find him there on June 23, 1668; but, full of musical designs as always, Mr. Pepys resolves "forthwith to have a little Harpsicon made me to confirm and help me in my musique notions, which my head is now-a-days full of. . . ." It is doubtful that Mr. Pepys ever mastered it; but, in addition to its ornamental place in his parlor, the harp-shaped instrument could be plucked, and it served as the focus of many of Mr. Pepys's musical sessions.

There was yet another musical instrument, closely related to the harpsichord, that Pepys tried to master: the triangle. It was not the modest piece of metal rattled with metal that country musicians play. It was a spinet, or virginal; Mr. Pepys owned one, and it furnished restful after-dinner activity as on Sunday, June 21, 1663: "went up and tried a little upon my tryangle, which I understand fully, and with a little use I believe could bring myself to do something." The little instrument gave Mr. Pepys many occasions to sit right close to Mary Ashwell, his wife's companion: "and so home again and up to teach Ashwell the grounds of time and other things on the tryangle, and made her take out a Psalm very well, she having a good ear and hand" (May 3, 1663). When the little spinet lost its proper tone, Mr. Pepys called on the virginal-maker on April 1, 1663; bought a rest to tune the instrument; took a craftsman home from the shop to show him how to use it; and resolved to tune the little spinet himself in the future. Moreover, he dignified it by "having a new frame made proper for it to stand on" on July 1, 1664.

Part-singing, composing or polishing songs, playing or practicing on various instruments, amateur musician Pepys delighted in sweet sounds and in attempts to attain virtuosity.

CHAPTER 9

A Puritan at the Theater

MR. Pepys's daily round of pleasures included not only music and other diversions but the theater. He went to see plays, good and bad, almost every time there was a change on the boards. Pepys went to the theater for all sorts of reasons, and he reported countless fascinating facts. In fact, no satisfactory study of the Restoration stage can be made without consulting the *Diary*.

There was a very strong Puritan vein in Mr. Pepys, despite conduct that may seem to the contrary; but the stresses and strains of daily living, the temptations of the flesh, and the mercurial ways of London gradually weakened his resolutions. Even though he dearly loved the theater and sometimes could be found there for several succeeding days, the young Clerk of the Acts harbored a feeling that it was downright sinful to attend plays. He had learned well the anti-theater Puritan strictures that had kept the theaters closed by law from 1642 until 1660: they were dens of iniquity, the Bible forbade men's wearing women's clothing, theaters were fire hazards, and diseases lurked in them.

I   His Anti-Theater Vows

All these complaints and others he remembered; but, truth to tell, he enjoyed looking at the actresses and he loved the audience, especially when the King was there with a little female moth or two fluttering around him and when Mr. Pepys rather self-consciously felt that eyes were turned on him at the theater. What he went to the theater for mainly, though, was to see the drama; otherwise, he would never have left such a careful account of so many plays. His conscience worried him, nevertheless, to the point where he made vows as to deadlines within which he simply would not go to the theater; and, when he broke his vows, he paid into the poor box money that he kept in his house for the purpose. His moral reservations of October 21, 1661, though a little more pointed than usual, express definitely how he felt: "and so against my judgment and conscience (which God forgive, for my heart knows that I offend God in breaking my vows herein) to the Opera, which is now newly begun to act again, after some alteration of their scene, which do make it very much worse, but the play 'Love and Honour,' being the first time of their acting it, is a very good plot, and well done." He went to see the same play three times within a week: on October 21, 23, and 25. On the 26th he saw the Duke of Newcastle's *The Country Captain*, "but so silly a play as in all my life I never saw," Pepys complained.

After he had listened to a dull sermon lasting more than an hour in Spital Square on April 2, 1662, Mr. Pepys sought diversion at the Opera, the Duke's Theater. Here, with Mrs. Pepys, he enjoyed a favorite play, Philip Massinger's *The Bondman*. He made a resolution, nevertheless, to see no more plays until Whitsuntide, some fifty days past Easter. He broke his resolution on May 7 when he stepped into the King's Theater, no doubt without paying, in time to catch the last act of Beaumont and Fletcher's *The Knight of the Burning Pestle*.

Whitsuntide passing on May 18, Mr. Pepys saw John Fletcher's comedy, *The Night Walker* or *The Little Thief* on May 19, the second part of Sir William Davenant's heroic play *The Siege of Rhodes* the following night, the Duke of Newcastle's *The French Dancing Master* on the next night, and James Shirley's *Love in a Maze* the night after that. Four nights in a row he had seen four different plays, and his mounting enthusiasm was whetted by the famous comedian John Lacey's acting in the last two. On the very next night, May 23, Pepys admits: "my Lord [Sandwich] and I slunk away to the Opera, where we saw *Witt in a Constable*, but found it so silly a play as he had ever seen in his life." Rejoining Mrs. Pepys, he then went to see a puppet play in Covent Garden, finding it very pleasant. He had seen two performances in a single day.

At Michaelmas, September 29, 1662, Mr. Pepys escorted his wife and Margaret Penn to the King's Theater to see Shakespeare's *A Midsummer Night's Dream*. Some good dancing and the sight of some handsome women were all the pleasure he conceded. A visit next day to the Duke's Theater especially to see the great actor Thomas Betterton in John Webster's *The Duchess of Malfi* showed Mr. Pepys how easy it was for him to revert to his love of plays, and he vowed to quit them until Christmas.

Cheating on his vows a little, and pardonably, he fell in step on October 2, behind a group of gentlemen going through a private door into the Cockpit. He had heard that the King and Queen and other fine folk would be there to see James Shirley's *The Cardinal*, but he did not think much of the performance.

Mr. Tom Porter's new play *The Villain* had been so much talked about—Mr. Killigrew,[1] Captain Ferrers,[2] and Dr. Clarke having praised it highly within twenty-four hours—that Mr. Pepys went to the Duke's Theater to see it on October 20; and he confessed to the *Diary* that he was never less pleased with a play in his life. He added that, although there were good singing and dancing, there was no "fancy" in the play. He loved fancy—sparks of imagination and clever contrivance in a play—as well as heightened language to match the action or, for that matter, whatever it is that brings a play to life, including good and proper acting. Mr. Pepys was having other worries on October 20, however; his conscience bothered him: "I ought not to have gone by my vow, and, besides, my business commanded me elsewhere." As soon as he came home he paid five shillings to the poor box, according to his vow, and soothed his conscience with the thought: "I thank God these pleasures are not sweet to me now in the very enjoying of them."

For some time thereafter he kept his anti-theater vows quite well since he had been tempted, had heard news of the theater, and had even bought and read part of George Chapman's *Bussy d'Ambois* on November 15. When Mr. Pepys went to the Cockpit on November 17, he shifted the responsibility for his going to John Creed's shoulders, saying that Creed "carried" Mrs. Pepys and him. What really urged him, however, was the fact that he had learned earlier that day at Whitehall Palace that a royal party was going to see Beaumont and Fletcher's *The Scornful Lady*. "We had excellent places, and saw the King, Queen, Duke of Monmouth, his son, and my Lady Castlemaine,[3] and all the fine ladies," purred Mr. Pepys, adding that the play was well performed. He did not mind that the performance lasted until eleven o'clock, "it being fine moonshine."

The theater tempted Mr. Pepys. He read Fletcher's *A Wife for a Month* on December 19, and on December 26 mused: "But, Lord! to consider how my natural desire is to pleasure, which God be praised that he has given me the power by my late oaths to curb so well as I have done, and will do again after two or three plays more." The situation that led to this rationalizing was his visit that day to the Duke's Theater to see Thomas Parker's *The Villain* that he had condemned and had paid for seeing by a contribution to the poor box on October 20. Mr. Pepys seemed to like the play no better this time, but he observed that he ought not see a play without taking his wife.

He kept this half-hearted resolution by taking Mrs. Pepys to see the second part of Sir William Davenant's *Siege of Rhodes* the following day, but the Duke's Theater "was full of citizens, there hardly being a gentleman or woman in the house"; moreover, prentices were jostling the few pretty ladies present. Of the two or three plays that he had promised to see before resuming his vows, one was *The Villain* that he had recently condemned. After seeing it on New Year's Day, 1663, Pepys admitted chagrin for having undervalued the play. He found it this time to be good and pleasant and "an allowable tragedy." The house was full of citizens; hence, the occasion was less pleasant, said Pepys, who promised to stop his "gaddings" and stick to business for the year; but he broke this New Year resolution four days later when he went to see Thomas Killigrew's *Claracilla*, "a poor play," at the King's Theater.

Twelfth Day, January 6, 1663, an important ending-date for the Christmas holidays, seemed to Mr. Pepys to be an appropriate day to go to the theater to see Shakespeare's *Twelfth Night*; and after he had seen and praised Sir Samuel Tuke's old play *The Adventures of Five Hours* at the Duke's Theater on January 8, Mr. Pepys resolved to see no more plays until Easter or, perhaps, until Whitsuntide; but he left a loophole: "excepting plays at court." *The Adventures of Five Hours* tempted him to the theater on January 17, nevertheless; and, though he was out of sorts, he still thought the play very fine. Perhaps trifling with his vows was induced by a birthday mood since Mr. Pepys observed on February 23, 1663, that he was thirty years of age, and he saw two plays: Sir Robert Stapylton's *The Slighted Maid* and John Dryden's *Wild Gallant*. In the former, he enjoyed the little girl's fine legs which only "bends in the hams." And, although the latter was well acted, he regarded it as a poor play, especially since there was so little in it that substantiated the title. He was somewhat mollified, nevertheless, by a satisfying view of His Majesty; of Lady Castlemaine, whose reputation was becoming precipitately notorious; and of others of His Majesty's ladies, in-

cluding Mrs. Wells, who had returned to court after surviving
the vile experience of being believed to have been the very lady
who had dropped a child during a court ball a few days before.

To be close to King and Court always thrilled Mr. Pepys.
When he saw the King and his courtiers going to the Duke's
Theater on December 22, 1663, to see Shakespeare's *Henry VIII,*
Mr. Pepys almost joined them; but he would have broken his
oath, "or run the hazard of 20s losse" to the poor box. He was
tempted again to see the play on Christmas Eve, but resisted until New Year's Day.

Mr. Pepys's New Year's resolution included a carefully hedged
vow regarding the theater: he would see not more than one play
a month at any public theater and not spend more than fifty
shillings; if spent, he would see none before next New Year's
Day. In matters of conscience-plus-money Mr. Pepys would leave
a loophole; in this instance, the loophole was "unless that I do
become worth £1000 sooner than then, and then am free to
come to some other terms." Vows made, he went, on January 2
to see Edward Howard's *The Usurper,* which, said Pepys, was
not a good play but was better than the one he had seen yester-
day, Shakespeare's *Henry VIII.* During this same month, Mr.
Pepys who had once started to write a play, found on January
30, 1664, while going through old papers, the pages of his unfinished effort *Love a Cheat.* He had started it ten years ago at
Cambridge, and, reading it, he liked it very much but doubted
that he could do so well now if he tried.

When he saw Sir William Davenant's play *The Unfortunate
Lovers* at the Duke's Theater on March 7, Mr. Pepys thought
that he had perhaps become more critical of plays than formerly
or that the nearly empty theater dampened his enthusiasm. He
struggled with his conscience, too, for the next day he found it
necessary to justify going to the theater to see Ludovic Carlell's
Heraclius or The Emperor of the East (translated from Corneille). Pepys's part of the dialogue with his conscience included
the argument that there would be no plays at Court during the
Lenten season; and, continuing, Pepys stated that it was only for
the saving of time and money that he made his vows. He van-
quished his conscience on this occasion by resolving to pay a
forfeit to the poor box, and concluded, "I do not find myself in
the least apprehensive that I have done any violence to my
oaths." Thus defying his conscience, Mr. Pepys enjoyed the play.

So often did Mr. Pepys break his vows against theater-going that it was no wonder that on November 28, 1667, Sir Richard Browne criticized him for going so often to see plays. Sir Richard told him that he was surprised to see a man of so much business at the theater. Pepys grumbled to himself that, indeed, he deserved being thought a busy man but had now come to be censured with his fellow navy officials for a man of negligence. This censure did not keep him away from the theater, however; for Pepys saw Shakespeare's *Tempest* at the Duke's on December 12, but he would not look around "for fear of being seen." He commented, nevertheless, on a scantily clad French lady who did not look decent.

Continuing to go to the theater and to enjoy himself, despite all, Mr. Pepys had an amusing encounter with the orange woman at the Duke of York's playhouse on May 11, 1668, between the acts of Shakespeare's *Tempest*. She out-talked Mr. Pepys, claiming that at a night play he had recently ordered her to deliver oranges to some ladies in a box, but had not paid for them. To quiet the hoyden, he had to purchase four shillings worth of oranges on the spot. Between the occasion of Sir Richard Browne's soft indictment on November 28, 1667, and the encounter with the orange girl, Mr. Pepys had gone to the theater to see at least thirty-nine performances and to suffer an occasional prick of conscience.

Hoping to find Mr. Pepys at the King's Theater, his wife, Elizabeth, and the little maid Deborah Willet had gone there on June 19, 1668. They had not found him at the theater nor did Mrs. Pepys approve of John Dryden's play *An Evening's Love or The Mock Astrologer*. Mr. Pepys took her alone to see the play next day but he, too, criticized it for "being very smutty," and not so good as the playwright's heroic plays *The Indian Emperor* and *The Maiden Queen*.[4]

Despite his vows to the contrary, Mr. Pepys gave his patronage to theaters for the remaining summer days. He went to the King's or to the Duke's Theater as the play, as the quest for sport or other inducement, led him. He saw Thomas Shadwell's *The Sullen Lovers or The Impertinents*[5] at the Duke's Theater on June 24; Dryden's *The Indian Queen* at the King's Theater on the 27th. And Pepys noted that at the King's Theater, on July 11, in James Shirley's play *Hyde Park*, horses were brought upon the stage.

There is evidence enough to show that one reason for Mr. Pepys's current fervid theater-going was that little Deb, Mrs. Pepys's maid, usually went with them and Pepys was currently fondling her. In any event, Mr. Pepys saw plays on July 17, 29, 31, August 1 and 5; and at the Duke's Theater on August 12 he saw Shakespeare's *Macbeth* "to our great content," he reported. Having seen other plays between times, he reported that on August 31, he, Mrs. Pepys, Deb, and others saw Shakespeare's *Hamlet* and were "mightily pleased with it." On September 4, Mr. Pepys saw an old favorite, Ben Jonson's *Bartholomew Fair* "with puppets"; and he observed current shifting political winds with the statement that he objected to anti-Puritan strictures in the play: "The business of abusing the Puritans begin to grow stale, and of no use, they being the people that, at last, will be found the wisest." The rise of the Puritans was, indeed, a political reality in the seventeenth century.

II *Shakespeare and the Cavalier Playwrights*

Mr. Pepys did not entirely approve of Shakespeare as a playwright, but both men belonged to the same century and the idolatrous regard of "The Bard" was far in the future. He generally approved *Hamlet*, and when he saw it performed at the Opera, the Duke of York's theater in Lincoln's Inn Fields, on August 24, 1661, he thought it was "done with scenes very well"; "but above all," he added, "Betterton did the prince's part beyond imagination." Mr. Pepys, inadvertently, started to list the famous actors who had starred in the role of Hamlet. Seeing *Hamlet* again at the King's Theater on November 27, 1661, Mr. Pepys conceded that the play was very well done. During the years of the *Diary* he saw the famous tragedy at other times: on December 5, 1661; May 28, 1663; and August 31, 1668. The famous actor Thomas Betterton made the play succeed, for Pepys, who was always praising him, stating on August 31 that he was mightily pleased with the play, "but, above all, with Betterton, the best part, I believe, that ever man acted." Mr. Pepys, no doubt, was also one of the first of tens of thousands who have committed to memory Hamlet's soliloquy. On Sunday, November 13, 1664, he spent all afternoon indoors with Mrs. Pepys committing " 'To bee or not to bee' without book."

He did not have too exalted an opinion of other plays of Shakespeare that he saw at the theaters or read at home. Mr. Pepys records that on December 31, 1660, he bought *Henry IV* (part I) at Paul's Churchyard; that he went to the New Theater to see it acted; but that, his expectation being too great, it did not please him as, otherwise, he thought it would. And he added that, having the book, he believed, did spoil the play a little. What Mr. Pepys was doing, probably, during the play was following the action on stage by reading from his newly bought copy.

He admitted on June 4, 1661, nevertheless, that the "Harry the 4th" that he had seen at the King's Theater that day was "a good play." His opinion of the play declined sharply on November 2, 1667, for in the intervening years Mr. Pepys had seen scores of plays and, truth to tell, his critical opinion of Shakespeare's play had declined. On this date, he confessed that, contrary to expectation, he was pleased in nothing more, in *Henry IV*, than in Falstaff's speech about "What is honour?" He saw parts of *Henry IV* again on January 7 and on September 8, 1668; on the former date he admitted not liking what he had seen, and on the latter expressed no opinion, probably because he had stepped into the King's Theater only at the end of the performance because he had hoped to go out with the actress Mrs. Knepp. It was too late, however, and she had to study her part in Ben Jonson's *Epicoene* for next day's performance.

Mr. Pepys's critical estimate of Shakespeare's *Henry VIII*, although not high, followed an opposite course to his views on *Henry IV*; for his estimate seemed to improve, though not too much. On December 10, 1663, Mr. Wooten, the shoemaker, had told Pepys that *Henry VIII* "with all his wives, a rare play," would be acted that week; and on December 22 Mr. Pepys observed that the King, the Duke of York, and the Court were going to the Duke's Theater to see the performance, "which is said to be an admirable play." Admitting that, because of his antitheater vows, this would be his first play in six months, Mr. Pepys, on January 1, 1664, went to see "the much cried up play of Henry the Eighth." He had gone with the resolution of liking the play, stated Pepys, but it turned out to be "so simple a thing made up of a great many patches, that, besides the shows and processions in it, there [was] nothing in the world good or well done" in the performance. He commented casually on *Henry VIII* on January 27, saying that public opinion was that John

Dryden's new play *The Indian Queen* was better than *Henry VIII*. By December 30, 1668, however, Mr. Pepys's evaluation of Shakespeare's play had improved. Seeing it at the Duke's Theater, he was more highly pleased than he expected with its history and pageantry.

Shakespeare's native scenes in *The Merry Wives of Windsor* should have pleased Mr. Pepys, but it was the acting that he seemed to disapprove. When he saw the play on December 5, 1660, Pepys stated that the parts of the country gentleman and of the French doctor were very well done "but the rest but very poorly and Sir J. Falstaffe as bad as any." His opinion of the play did not improve when he saw it on September 25, 1661, when he found it "ill done"; nor again, on August 15, 1667, when he stated that no part of the play pleased him.

While walking through Lincoln's Inn Fields on September 11, 1661, Mr. Pepys learned that a new play, Shakespeare's *Twelfth Night or What You Will*, was being presented at the Opera and that the King was there. Against his will, Pepys went into the theater and found no pleasure at all in the play. When he saw it again on January 6, 1663, he called it a silly play and pointed out that there was no relationship between its title and action. And on January 20, 1669, seeing *Twelfth Night* at the Duke's Theater he still judged it to be one of the weakest plays that he had ever seen.

If Shakespeare's play *The Tempest* fared somewhat better in his judgment, it was because an item in the play caught his fancy: the Echo Song in which Ferdinand sings to himself and Ariel echoes him. On November 7, 1667, when he saw the play Mr. Pepys commented on "this curious piece of musique in an echo of half sentences, the echo repeating the former half. . . ."

During a performance of *The Tempest* on May 11, 1668, Pepys had tried to write down the words of the song, but his copy was blurred and after the play Henry Harris, the actor, had dictated the words to him. From a somewhat tentative judgment of *The Tempest* that the play had "no great wit, but yet good, above ordinary plays" on November 7, 1667, Pepys proceeded, on November 13, to a more favorable evaluation that the play was very pleasant and so full of good variety that he could not be more pleased with a comedy. He felt, nevertheless, that the seamen's part was a little too tedious. Variety—the Echo Song, the seamen's dance, the actors in their several costumes, the droll situations—

all helped to make *The Tempest* one of the better plays of Shakespeare in Mr. Pepys's judgment; and he saw it on nine occasions between November 7, 1667, and January 21, 1669.

Maintaining no steady adulation for Shakespeare as a playwright, Mr. Pepys went to the theater to see many of his plays: *Hamlet, Henry IV* (I), *Henry VIII, Macbeth, Othello, Romeo and Juliet, The Merry Wives of Windsor, The Tempest, A Midsummer Night's Dream*, the altered versions of *Measure for Measure* and *The Taming of the Shrew*. Pepys recorded his opinion of the foregoing plays and he saw most of them more than once. The one he liked least was *A Midsummer Night's Dream* which he went to see at the King's Theater on September 29, 1662; he concluded that it was "the most insipid ridiculous play" that he had ever seen. Another early critical opinion hardly more favorable concerned *Romeo and Juliet*. When Mr. Pepys saw the play at the Opera on March 1, 1662, he dceided that it was the worst play that he had ever heard in his life and the worst acted. He resolved never to go again to see a play on opening night.

As the years passed, Mr. Pepys's critical judgment became more discriminating; and he gave Shakespeare higher, if often grudging, praise. Audience, acting, contrivance, theme, and the interplay of fancy molded Pepys's opinion of a play. All led him to value Shakespeare's *Macbeth* which he went to see at the Duke's Theater on January 7, 1667, as "a most excellent play in all respects. . . ."

Ben Jonson fared better than Shakespeare in Pepys's opinion of plays. He thought Jonson's *Epicoene or the Silent Woman* that he saw at the King's Theater on January 7, 1661, "an excellent play." On one of the many occasions that he saw the play, June 1, 1664, at the King's Theater, Pepys complained that it was not so well acted nor so good a play as formerly he thought it to be; but, in fact, it was one of his favorites. Thinking no doubt of Jonson's theory of "humours," Mr. Pepys thought that his own "humour" caused today's disaffection.

Jonson's *The Alchemist* in Pepys's judgment was "a most incomparable play." He went to see it at the King's Theater on June 22, 1661; in similar language he evaluated Jonson's *Bartholomew Fair*. Observing that the play was acted for the first time since the theaters were reopened, Mr. Pepys stated on June 8, 1661, that the play was "most admirable." He objected, nevertheless, that it was "too much prophane and abusive." When he saw the play at the King's Theater on September 7, 1661, Mr. Pepys objected to the introduction of puppets and to harsh anti-Puritan strictures in the play. He observed, further, that no one had dared present the play during the forty-year rise of the Puritans and he wondered that even now the King would countenance its performance. *Bartholomew Fair* was "the best comedy in the world," thought Mr. Pepys, when he saw it at the King's Theater on August 2, 1664; and, despite an occasional objection, he always enjoyed it. High in Mr. Pepys's estimate stood also Jonson's *Volpone or The Fox*; seeing it at the King's Theater on January 14, 1665, Pepys thought that it was "a most excellent play . . . and well-acted."

When Mr. Pepys read Jonson's tragedy *Catiline* on Sunday, December 18, 1664, he called it "a very excellent piece"; and he was glad to hear, three years later (December 7, 1667) that the play would soon be acted. Some difficulties intervened in assembling a sufficiently impressive company of actors, adequate scenery, and the magnificent costumes that the play required. When the performance finally opened at the King's Theater on December 19, 1668, Mr. Pepys gave approval to certain scenes and concluded that the play "is only to be read."

"Propriety of speech" in a play was one of Mr. Pepys's dramatic criteria, and he was satisfied with Jonson's fulfillment of it in *Every Man in His Humour* that Pepys read on February 9, 1667. Jonson's comedy of "humours" was more in style on the Restoration stage than Shakespeare's comedy of fanciful invention. The comedy of manners that came to be the vogue in the Restoration theater was the natural outcome of Jonsonian "humour," and in the theater Mr. Pepys felt more comfortable in Jonson's presence than in Shakespeare's.

The most readily available plays for reopening of the theaters in 1660 were, obviously, those written for the Elizabethan and Jacobean stage; plays written or reworked by such theater entrepreneurs as Sir William Davenant and Thomas Killigrew, or by the aging Cavaliers, including Sir Samuel Tuke and Sir William Killigrew; adaptations from playwrights Corneille, Molière, and others of the thriving Théâtre Française; plays written while the theaters were presumably closed such as Abraham Cowley's *Cutter of Coleman Street*, written in 1658 against the day when the theaters would legally reopen, surely; and whatever drolls, recitatives, and interludes were showing in the newly opened theaters. Mr. Pepys went to see them all and established many plays as his favorites. Beaumont and Fletcher's plays were among those he saw most frequently—at least twenty by these famous partners, and most of them many times over.

On almost every occasion that he saw a play Mr. Pepys gave a thoughtful appraisal of it; and, as his critical judgment developed, he wrote in the *Diary* something more explicit than a mere statement of approval or disapproval. It will suffice to cite a few instances from Beaumont and Fletcher's plays to demonstrate his development as a critic. He liked *The Mad Lover* "pretty well" on February 9, 1661; he thought *A King and No King* "well acted" on March 14, and "very well done" on September 26; he found *Philaster* far short of his expectations on November 18; and "little good" in *The Humorous Lieutenant* on May 8, 1663. Mr. Pepys's critical judgment sharpening, he saw the then famous *The Wildgoose Chase* for the first time on January 11, 1668. With such an intriguing title and with such fame, the play, Mr. Pepys thought, should have been better contrived and more pertinently developed. He condemned it: "for in this play I met with nothing extraordinary at all, but very dull inventions and designs."

III   *Pepys as Critic*

Quite reasonably, Mr. Pepys thought that the most important requirement for a successful play was good acting, and he commented frequently on the actors and their performance. "A good play and well-performed" was his entry in the *Diary* on February 18, 1662, after he had seen Sir William Davenant's *The Law Against Lovers.* Moreover, good acting could improve even a mediocre play, he stated, for Davenant's *The Rivals* was "no excellent play but [had] good acting in it." On May 1, 1667, he saw James Shirley's *The Changes* or *Love in a Maze* at the King's Theater and called it "a sorry play" but commended John Lacy's acting as "most admirable, indeed." Conversely, Mr. Pepys condemned many plays for poor acting and the actors for their behavior.

At the Duke of York's Theater with Mrs. Pepys to see Ludovic Carlell's *Heraclius,* on September 5, 1667, Mr. Pepys was disgusted by the actors' beastly laughing, clowning, and forgetting their parts; and he thought that their behavior was induced by the scanty but noisy audience. Mr. Pepys, who respected the theater as an institution, was ashamed of the way it was being debased.

Mr. Pepys admired a well-written play, and he praised the "extraordinary good contrivance" of Beaumont and Fletcher's *The Humorous Lieutenant* that he saw at the Theater Royal on May 8, 1663. One of his highly favored plays was Philip Massinger's tragedy *The Bondman*; and, when Pepys stated on July 28, 1664, that "there is nothing more taking in the world with me than that play," he meant that in his judgment it was well written. He had bought the play at Paul's Churchyard on May 25, 1661; stated on November 21, 1661, that the more often he read the play the better he liked it; called it on March 1, 1661, "an excellent play and well done"; praised it highly again on March 19; caught the last act at the Opera on November 25; and, again, on April 2, 1662, praised this play by stating that at the Opera he saw *The Bondman* most excellently acted and that he had never liked it better.

Although Mr. Pepys was an amateur theater critic and never aspired to be professional, he followed a procedure that any critic in any age should adopt. As in the case of *The Bondman*, he bought the play, read it many times, saw it at the theater on numerous occasions, and, on the basis of intimate knowledge, drew his conclusions concerning the play.

IV *Favorite Actors and Actresses*

The actors performing in the play often induced Mr. Pepys to a favorable critical conclusion. He had his special favorites, none exceeding Thomas Betterton. Pepys stated on March 1, 1661: "but above all that I ever saw Betterton do the Bondman the best"; and he praised his acting in the same play on March 19 and on November 4, calling him "the best actor in the world." Betterton played the Prince in *Hamlet* "beyond imagination" at the Opera on August 24, 1661, and again the actor, playing the same part on May 28, 1663, at the Duke's Theater, gave Mr. Pepys "fresh reason never to think enough of Betterton." And when, on October 16, 1667, Mr. Pepys went to the Duke's Theater to see Betterton in *Macbeth*, he was "vexed to see Young (who is but a poor actor) at best act Macbeth in the room of Betterton, who, poor man! is sick"; "but, Lord what a prejudice it wrought in me against the whole play, and everybody else agreed in disliking this fellow." Mr. Betterton, who regained his health, continued to delight his audience; and his acting in many plays thrilled Mr. Pepys who stated his belief that, Betterton, playing the lead in *Hamlet* at the Duke's Theater, on August 31, 1668, played "the best part that ever man acted."

Henry Harris came near to Thomas Betterton in reputation as an actor. He came to be a close dining friend and musical companion of Pepys; for, like Pepys, he had a good singing voice. On July 20, 1664, Mr. Pepys saw Harris at the Duke's Theater in the Earl of Bristol's *Worse and Worse* and conceded that he began to admire him more than ever as an actor. Teamed with Betterton, and with Mrs. Betterton playing Ianthe, Harris played the part of King Henry in Lord Orrery's *Henry V* at the Duke's Theater on August 13, 1664, and his acting, that of his distinguished partners, and the entire performance earned Mr. Pepys's high critical praise: "a most noble play . . . wherein Betterton, Harris, and Ianthe's parts are most incomparably wrote and done, and the whole play the most full of height and raptures of wit and sense, that ever I heard." Betterton, his wife, and Mr. Harris won Pepys's commendation again, acting in Sir William Davenant's play *The Rivals* at the Duke's Theater on December 2, 1664; and Harris's performances and friendship continued to delight Mr. Pepys.

Although no other actor won Betterton's or Harris's high place in Pepys's esteem, there were others who pleased him on occasion: young Edward Kynaston in the part of the Duke's sister in Beaumont and Fletcher's *The Loyal Subject* at the Cockpit on August 18, 1660, delighted Pepys; and Kynaston pleased him in other plays also. Michael Mohun, who came with a great reputation to the English stage with King Charles from France, and whose acting in James Shirley's *The Traitor* on November 22, 1660, at the new theater in Lincoln's Inn Fields won Pepys's approval also won high rating. And Charles Hart played "most excellently" in James Howard's *The Mad Couple* at the King's Theater on December 28, 1667, in what Pepys thought "but an ordinary play."

John Lacy was Mr. Pepys's favorite comedian. Pepys concluded after seeing James Shirley's *The Changes* or *Love in a Maze* at the Royal Theater on June 10, 1663: "The play is pretty good, but the life of the play is Lacy's part, the clown, which, is

most admirable. . . ." Lacy played the comic part of the Irish
footman in Sir Robert Howard's anti-Puritan play *The Committee* "beyond imagination" at the same theater two days later; and
the comedian delighted Mr. Pepys when he played the same part
on other occasions and acted in comic parts in many other plays.

The introduction of actresses upon the Restoration stage delighted Mr. Pepys and many won his critical approval: Mrs.
Betterton; Mrs. Coleman, the musician's wife; Anne and Rebecca
Marshall, sisters; Mary Davis, who took King Charles's fancy;
and Mrs. Knepp, who took Pepys's and became his intimate
friend. Each of these and others won on occasion his praise and
his critical judgment convinced him that women playing female
parts would be more convincing.

The best-known and probably the best of Restoration actresses
was Ellen Gwyn. Rumor and some evidence assign her a prominent place among King Charles's many mistresses. Mr. Pepys has
left abundant contributions in the *Diary* to "Nell" Gwyn's reputation on and off stage; and, no doubt about it, she was a convincing performer, especially in comic parts. Pepys stated after
seeing her on March 2, 1667, at the King's Theater, in the part
of Florimell in Dryden's play *The Maiden Queen*: "I never can
hope ever to see the like done again, by man or woman . . . so
great performance of a comical part was never, I believe, in the
world before as Nell do this. . . ." With an occasional exception,
she continued to draw superlatives from Mr. Pepys for many
roles.

V *The Play off-Stage*

Every time, almost, that Mr. Pepys went to the theater something interesting happened to him off-stage. The average theater-
goer would be expected to buy his ticket, take his place in the
theater, and look at the performance. Although Pepys did these
things, he also gazed at his aristocratic betters, especially King,
Court, and court ladies; he flirted with the ladies about him and
paid other attentions to them; he cocked his ear to catch current
gossip; and he witnessed often the type of incident that happens
once in a lifetime, if then, in an average man's presence. At the
Cockpit, on April 20, 1661, to see Beaumont and Fletcher's tragi-
comedy *The Humorous Lieutenant*, Pepys records a typical reaction: "But my pleasure was great to see the manner of it, but
above all Mrs. Palmer, with whom the King do discover a great

imitated himself, there being much the same scenes and contrivances in his current play as in his plays *Henry V* and *Mustapha.* The audience became bored and restless during the reading of a long letter, part of the action, and hooted and hissed; and Mr. Pepys believed that, had not His Majesty been present, the audience would have hissed the play off the stage. He descanted at length on the fifteen-minute-long letter, noted Lord Berkeley's standing comments on the playwright's stupidity, and laughed all the way home and until bedtime, especially when Mrs. Pepys expressed anger at his and the audience's laughing at a play in the King's presence.

The action off-stage was really dramatic on November 2: "a gentleman of good habit, sitting just before us, eating of some fruit in the midst of the play, did drop down as dead, being choked; but with much ado Orange Moll did thrust her finger down his throat, and brought him to life again." The action off-stage involved Mr. Pepys directly at the King's Theater on January 28, 1661; "and here I sitting behind in a dark place, a lady spit backward upon me by a mistake, not seeing me, but after seeing her to be a very pretty lady, I was not troubled at it at all."

VI   *Theater Historian*

Since Mr. Pepys went to the theater for many reasons, he has reported countless fascinating facts. Pepys comments frequently on the general improvement in dress in the Restoration audience. And on May 8, 1663, he was a little ashamed that Mrs. Pepys and her attendant had been "in such a pickle" at the theater while all the ladies were finer and better dressed in the pit than they used to be. He comments often, too, on the continuing bad manners in the theater—the buzzing conversation, fidgeting, soliciting by prostitutes, hawking of fruit by the orange girls, and the reintroduction of masks, probably lending mystery and suggestiveness to the ladies who wore them. On June 12, 1663, Lady Mary Cromwell, daughter of the Protector, came to the theater well dressed; and, when the house began to fill, she put on her mask. Pepys observed that masking had of late "become a great fashion among the ladies, which hides their whole face."

Seeing Beaumont and Fletcher's *Beggar's Bush* at the Theater on January 3, 1661, Pepys reported that for the first time he had seen women come upon the stage. He would see them in practically all female parts thereafter, but prior to the reopening of the theaters in 1660 all female parts were played by males, usually boys before their piping voices changed, and boys continued to play some female parts on the Restoration stage. Pepys returned a few days later, January 8, but withheld comment on the actresses, probably because the comedy *The Widow* by Jonson, Fletcher, and Middleton was "an indifferent play, but wronged by the women being to seek in their parts." His comment on the ladies is cryptic, but by February 12, Pepys gave full approval, saying that the part of the Scornful Lady in Beaumont and Fletcher's comedy of that name at the King's Theater, "now done by a woman," made the play appear much better than before. A play that had displeased him previously, Henry Glapthorne's *Argalus and Parthenia* won his approval at the King's Theater on October 28, 1661, "where a woman acted Parthenia, and came afterwards on the stage in men's clothes, and had the best legs that ever I saw, and I was very well pleased with it." The actresses continued to win Mr. Pepys's critical approval.

Many entries in the *Diary* attest to Mr. Pepys's interest in theater construction and to his keen and generally sound comments on theater architecture. Attending the newly opened Theater Royal in Drury Lane on October 8, 1663, Pepys observed its architectural faults such as the narrowness of the passages in and out of the pit, and the distance from the stage to the boxes, which would make it difficult for boxseat holders to hear the actors. Above all, he was displeased because the orchestra was located too far below the stage: "most of it sounding under the very stage," and the basses could not be heard at all nor the trebles very well." These comments indicate that Mr. Pepys knew not only plays and their contents but also whatever contributed to an effective theater performance.

Scenery in the Elizabethan and Jacobean theater was sparse and, at best, symbolic or representational; and scenery was also sparse on the early Restoration stage. Pepys records, however, substantial improvements in scenery. On July 2, 1661, noting that this was the fourth day since the opening of Sir William Davenant's new theater, the Opera, Pepys observed that upon the arrival of King Charles and the Queen of Bohemia the scene at the opening of the play was "very fine and magnificent." And on August 15, at the same theater, he saw Davenant's comedy *The Wits*, "never acted yet with scenes"; and, again, on August

24, at the same theater he remarked that *Hamlet* was performed "with scenes very well."

Scenery that was coming rapidly to be a part of Restoration staging continued to draw Pepys's notice: he commented on "the shows and processions" in Shakespeare's *Henry VIII* at the Duke's Theater on January 1, 1664, and referred on December 30, 1668, again to the "shows" in the play, referring to scenery, no doubt. It was only for "the scenes sake which is very fine indeed and worth seeing" that he went to see John Fletcher's *The Faithful Shepherdess* at the Theater Royal on May 13, 1663; and the "good scene of a town on fire" delighted him in Beaumont and Fletcher's *The Island Princess*, staged at the King's Theater on January 7, 1689. Indirectly, moreover, on August 2, 1664, Pepys observed the introduction of scenery and other novelties in the theater on the occasion of a conversation with the King's jester and playwright, Thomas Killigrew, who mentioned plans for a new theater "where," Pepys recorded, "we shall have the best scenes and machines . . . as is in Christendome."

Close to scenery came the elaboration of costumes on the Restoration stage, and Pepys often recorded his impressions of them in the *Diary*. He did not think very highly of Ben Jonson's tragedy *Catiline* as a play to be acted; but, when Pepys saw it at the King's Theater on December 19, 1668, he observed the fine costumes and the splendid scene of the senate. As for Ludovic Carlell's *Heraclius* or *The Emperor of the East*, that he saw at the theater on March 8, 1664, Pepys thought the scene with "the garments like Romans very well," and quite worth-while; and he specified that what he thought the finest of all was the tableau of "The Emperor and his people about him, standing in their fixed and different postures in their Roman habitts, above all that ever yet I saw at any of the theatres."

Mr. Pepys noticed, nevertheless, that when he saw the costumes backstage they lost much of the shine and glory that theater lights gave them. This fact and others concerning the bustling Restoration stage drew Pepys's amazed response on March 19, 1666: "to the King's playhouse, all in dirt, they being altering of the stage to make it wider . . . but my business here was to see the inside of the stage and all the tiring-rooms and machines; and, indeed, it was a sight worthy seeing. But to see their clothes, and the various sorts, and what a mixture of things there was; here a wooden leg, there a ruff, here a hobby horse, there a crown, would make a man split himself to see with laughing"; indeed he was shocked to see how poor seemed the costumes when bereft of footlights. It was candle light that was currently being used, Pepys recorded. He observed, too, how fine the machines were and how very pretty the paintings back-stage. Another novelty in the Restoration theater that Pepys noticed was the curtain; and he observed, when he saw *Heraclius* (March 8, 1664), that at the beginning of the play, the curtain was drawn up.

Preoccupied as he was with his own musical efforts, Mr. Pepys kept account in the *Diary* of the improved place that music came to enjoy in the Restoration theater. That splendid theater man, Mr. Thomas Killigrew, discoursed at length with Pepys on February 12, 1667, about the development of the English theater since the time of the late King Charles I and about how Killigrew had tried to introduce good music into the theater. Musician Pepys, himself, has left many accounts in the *Diary* of the general success of music on the stage; for musical scores, singing actors, and songs in plays absorbed his interest. It was the music combined with apt scenery and good contrivance that literally sickened him with delight at the King's Theater, on February 27, 1668, when he saw Massinger's and Dekker's *The Virgin Martyr*: "But that which did please me beyond anything in the whole world was the wind-musique when the angel comes down, which is so sweet that it ravished me, and indeed, in a word did wrap my soul so that it made me really sick, just as I have formerly been when in love with my wife."

Fighting a losing battle with his conscience and his vows, Mr. Pepys devoted himself to the Restoration theater; and he has left a vivid account of the plays that were presented, of actors and actresses, of audiences, of the appurtenances, and of his own part of the play of life off-stage in the bustling theater of his day.

CHAPTER 10

The Plague

WHEN he got home past nine on the night of June 7, 1665, Mrs. Pepys had not returned from the city; and this fact, the stifling heat, and the strange brightness in the air, which Mr. Pepys attributed to the excessive heat, caused him to pace about in the garden until past midnight. The chief cause of his uneasiness, however, was a closer contact with The Plague than any that he had had heretofore, and Mr. Pepys tells how he was affected: "This day, much against my will, I did in Drury Lane, see two or three houses marked with a red cross upon the doors, and 'Lord have mercy upon us' writ there; which was a sad sight to me, being the first of the kind that to my remembrance, I ever saw. It put me into an ill conception of myself and my smell, so that I was forced to buy some roll-tobacco to smell and to chaw, which took away the apprehension." This deodorant and medicine, who knows, may have played some part in keeping Mr. Pepys alive and well during the days ahead.

Almost daily, nowadays, the diarist commented on the spread of The Plague which struck wherever it would, being no respecter of persons. On June 10, he mentioned that it had entered the Old City of London, and in surprise and shock he noted that it had appeared at his good friend and neighbor's, Dr. Burnett, in Fenchurch Street; and he remarked how mightily troubled he was at its closeness to Seething Lane and in the home of a physician.

When he went to Whitehall on June 29, Mr. Pepys saw the ominous sight of the court full of wagons and people ready to go out of town, adding that the Mortality Bill had grown to two hundred and sixty seven, about ninety more than the last. The whole day was crowded with evidence of leave-taking; and, when he said goodbye to Sir William Coventry, Pepys expressed the opinion that, like others, he hoped the Duke of York had not gone to stay.

Despite The Plague, His Lordship, the Earl of Sandwich, home from sea, had an assignment for Mr. Pepys: his daughter, Jemimah, was nubile; would Mr. Pepys get busy and arrange a marriage with Sir George Carteret's son. Mr. Pepys, who approved the match, promised to speak to Sir George about it as though the idea had originated in his own mind. His Lordship especially liked the proposal that Mr. Pepys assume the genesis of the plan and then bring the young ones together and marry them off in no time, lest The Plague take one or the other away.

I *Pepys Plays Pandarus*

The proposed marriage between Jemimah, the Earl of Sandwich's daughter, and Sir George Carteret's son, Philip, was heartily approved by all, including the King and the Duke of York. Indeed, everyone concerned, except Miss Jem and Mr. Philip, was in a state of purring satisfaction. On July 14, when Mr. Pepys visited Sir George, he found himself caught in the agreeable web of Lady Jem's and Lady Carteret's purchases for the wedding. The bride-to-be had gone to her aunt's, Lady Wright's, at the country seat at Dagnams. Mr. Carteret was to visit her there tomorrow, and Lord Cupid, Mr. Samuel Pepys, offered to attend him so that he would not be alone among strangers. The ladies Montagu and Carteret glady accepted Mr. Pepys's offer, and he fluttered in sheer delight at Lady Carteret's munificence: the jewels, the trousseau, and the bedding she had bought.

He took next day a boat to Redriffe where Mr. Carteret was waiting for him at his father's residence; they then went to the ferry at Greenwich, crossed the water, and set out by coach to Dagnams. Mr. Carteret was nervous, simple, and unsophisticated; and Mr. Pepys felt quite superior. At Dagnams, Mr. Carteret was generally uncommunicative in the presence of Miss Montagu. Lord John Crew asked Mr. Pepys's consent to leave "the young people together tonight, to begin their amours, his staying being but to be little"; but Mr. Pepys advised against such a course "lest the lady might be too much surprised." Mr. Carteret was escorted to his room, and Mr. Pepys asked how he liked his bride-to-be. He liked her mightily, Mr. Carteret confided.

Thoroughly enjoying and exploiting to the fullest his role of adviser-in-marriage, Mr. Pepys ventured to make suggestions to

Lady Wright and to Lord Crewe about the niceties of nuptial procedure. On the next morning, Sunday, July 16, he walked an hour or two before church with Mr. Carteret and reported the professional session: "Here I taught him what to do: to take the lady always by the hand to lead her, and telling him that I would find opportunity to leave them two together, he should make these and these compliments, and also take a time to do the like to Lord Crew and Lady Wright. After I had instructed him, . . . my Lord Crew come down and family, the young lady among the rest; and so by coaches to church four miles off. . . ."

After church and after family dinner, fate and contrivance finally left the young couple alone. Mr. Carteret slowly acquired confidence, and by afternoon church time he was escorting his fiancée handsomely, handing her in and out of the coach with courtly finesse. Married in due time, the couple fared quite well; for Pepys reports on August 1 that the newlyweds were doing just fine, "but both red in the face . . . [and] enough pleased with their night's lodging."

II *Pepys's Pace Never Slackens*

With death all about him, Mr. Pepys had arranged a marriage, and in the silent gloomy city, the Clerk of the Acts went regularly to the navy office and transacted whatever business came before him with whatever man who brought it. He called frequently on Sir George Carteret, Treasurer of the Navy; and he went often to Deptford to consult with whichever fellow commissioner he could find, for there were a few who minded business: Mr. Pett and, occasionally, Sir William Batten. Although tavern keepers, like other men, helped swell the mortality rate during The Plague, Mr. Pepys was still able to find a pleasant inn open; and he occasionally stopped in with a friend or business acquaintance for a drink.

With The Plague raging everywhere, it took more than mere asking to get a man to go abroad after dark; for he might meet bearers carrying the dead to their burying place, or he might even stumble over a fresh corpse in the darkness. The boatmen were also afraid, for not only might a passenger keel over in the boat, but link boats bearing the dead might pass unsafely close to the boats bearing the living. Indeed, death was everywhere. Mr. Pepys reported on August 22: "I went away and walked to

Greenwich, in my way seeing a coffin with a dead body therein, lying in an open close belonging to Coome farme, which was carried out last night, and the parish have not appointed any body to bury it; but only set a watch there day and night, that no body should go thither or come thence, which is a most cruel thing: this disease making us more cruel to one another than if we are doggs."

But Mr. Pepys did not appear to be terrified by The Plague nor unduly obsessed with it. His life moved placidly along and he relished the incidents that took place about him as when he notes on August 3, 1665, the Sandwiches' and Carterets' anxiety to settle an inheritance for the newlyweds "for fear of death on either side." He also tells the story of Mr. John Wright's plague-ridden maid servant who had been removed to an outhouse but who had escaped through a window and run away. The nurse who had been appointed to care for her, knocking and receiving no answer, believed her dead and told Mr. Wright so. Mr. Wright had experienced great trouble in persuading nearby village gravediggers to bury the maid: "so he went home full of trouble, and in the way met the wench walking over the common, which frighted him worse than before; and was forced to send people to take her which he did. . . ."

They forced the sick girl into a pest-coach, drew the blinds, and sent the conveyance to a pest-house. And, then, Mr. Pepys adds a detail that was humorous, though grim: Sir Anthony Browne, his brother, and some gallants in a coach met the coach with its ghostly burden in a narrow lane. Sir Anthony's brother, thinking that some modest maiden was riding therein, stopped, pushed the curtains aside, and saw the ghostly sick girl who "stunk mightily." The coachman cried out for shame. Some bystanders told the young gallants the true circumstances, and Mr. Browne was so frightened that he almost died on the spot.

Mr. Pepys felt, as he walked the London streets, the presence of The Plague that had become a close personal tragedy for everyman whose daily experiences must have closely paralleled Pepys's. Since Pepys reported them all, his report of the tragedy is most authentic. As Mr. Pepys made the daily round, he encountered intimate, grievous little incidents of The Plague on every hand; at Westminster Hall on August 8 he heard that "poor Will that used to sell us ale at the Hall-door, his wife and three children died, all, . . . in a day," or so thought

Mr. Pepys. As he retraced his steps through the pestilence-ridden inner city, he feared that he might have contracted the disease and resolved to go thither no more.

On the following day he adds still another gruesome story: Alderman Bence had stumbled over a dead corpse in the street and, going home and telling his wife of the experience, "she at the fright, being with child, fell sicke and died of the plague."

III   *He Is Active in His Temporary Quarters*

A full day of business, August 22, helped to put these grim reminders out of Mr. Pepys's mind, and he liked his temporary office and quarters at Greenwich. Bustling off to Deptford, he worked there too and, despite the grimness of the times, managed to enjoy good food and good fun with pliable Mrs. Bagwell. But Pepys reported on August 31 that the increase in the mortality bill during the past week had been almost two thousand, bringing the general bill to seven thousand odd, six thousand of which were caused by The Plague. Then, to make matters worse, the true number would be closer to ten thousand, "partly from the poor that cannot be taken notice of and partly from the Quakers and others that will not have any bell ring for them." Mr. Pepys derived some comfort in the thought, at this month's end, that personally he was doing quite well, a statement qualified only by "an ague by being forced to go early and late to Woolwich" where Mrs. Pepys and her maids were sojourning.

In these drastic times who could blame Mr. Pepys if he worked only a little at his office and went, instead, to Captain Cocke's[1] "and there drank a cup of good drink"? Indulging his familiar habit of justifying himself, Mr. Pepys admitted on September 15 that he was willing to allow himself a drink in this Plague time since his physician was dead and his surgeon out of the way. Going home, he mused that this painful commuting could not continue with winter coming on, "for go every day to Woolwich I cannot, without endangering my life; and staying from my wife at Greenwhich is not handsome."

Full of business as ever, on the morning of September 16, 1665, Mr. Pepys walked, despite The Plague, to Greenwich, reading a play as he went. When he got to the Greenwich office, he discovered that Navy Commissioner Sir John Minnes had stolen a march on him and had gone to inspect the fleet. He had no right to do such a thing without talking first with Mr. Pepys, for Sir John, like a doting fool, had gone to the fleet to do no good but to proclaim himself an ass; for he could give no help to the Earl of Sandwich whose fleet was lying off the buoy of the Nore. Surely, Mr. Pepys had no objection to Sir John's making an ass of himself; what angered him was that Minnes had robbed him of the pomp and circumstance that would attend not only a Principal Officer's boarding the Earl of Sandwich's flagship, but also the first of the landlubber officers to board the flagship since the recent victories over the Dutch. His Lordship, moreover, was Mr. Pepys's Earl and blood-relative. What right, in hell, did Sir John Minnes have to do a thing like that! It is humanly excusable that Mr. Pepys was cursing mad.

Despite his troubles, he managed to have a good time. After spending the night at Captain Cocke's residence, Mr. Pepys got up in fine spirits on Sunday morning, September 17; and, before he left his room, he drew a music scale. During this vacation time, he had a mind to perfect himself in the scales in order to practice music composition. Going downstairs, he found Captain Cocke under the hand of the village barber, whom Mr. Pepys knew as a man of parts in things musical. The tonsorial artist offered to come that day after dinner with his violin to play a set of lyra-airs for Mr. Pepys, who gladly accepted, hoping to be merry thereby. Church time at hand, he and Captain Cocke went to church and found a configuration dear to his heart, for no man loved a good English country Sunday more: "a company of fine people . . . and a fine Church, and very good sermon, Mr. Plume being a very excellent schollar and preacher."

IV *His Lordship Has Difficulty with Prize Goods*

With Lord Brouncker, Mr. Pepys visited His Lordship's flagship, the *Prince*. When day broke on September 18, the sight of the fleet, above a hundred ships great and small, strung out in the morning mist was a very fine thing to behold; the flagships of each squadron were distinguished by their several flags on their main, fore, or mizen masts. Commissioners Lord Brouncker, Sirs William Batten, John Minnes, and Mr. Samuel Pepys felt the need to report to the Duke of Albemarle on the present condition of the fleet—especially in the light of the recent visits that Brouncker, Minnes, and Pepys had paid it.

In Lord Brouncker's coach they went, on September 30, to seek the Duke at Lambeth; and, observant and sensitive as ever to his surroundings as he traveled, Mr. Pepys exclaims: "But Lord! what a sad time it is to see no boats upon the River; and grass grows all up and down White Hall court, and nobody but poor wretches in the streets." At the meeting, the Duke of Albemarle showed them the latest mortality bill; the number of dead had increased by six hundred over the last record, and had now reached 8,297, of which 7,165 were attributed to The Plague. Mr. Pepys was grief-stricken, for he, like others, had believed that the recent cold spell had slowed the spread of the scourge.

Business had to go on, nevertheless, and during the meeting Mr. Pepys detected collusion among the other commissioners who proposed to the Duke that two teams be appointed to take inventory of the prize ships: Lord Brouncker and Captain Cocke, a merchant representative, were to go as one team, and Sir John Minnes, joined by Sir George Smith as a merchant representative, as the other. Mr. Pepys objected that it would be a disservice to the King to appoint the merchants. "I did order it so that Lord Brouncker and Sir J. Minnes were ordered, but I did stop the merchants to be added . . . ," he asserts.

The passing days in September and October, 1665, were most difficult for all concerned, but particularly for His Lordship, the Earl of Sandwich. England was in desperate need of money; her citizens in London and its environs were suffering from starvation; death roamed the streets; and the wounded sailors were lying about the doorways, too sick and weak to mutiny. Everywhere there was distress, and honest men who had fought to win the rich prize goods, brought by ships to England, were begging bread in the streets. But His Lordship and a few avaricious commanders had stolen the prize goods and were lining their pockets with golden angels quickly tendered by greedy merchants. Had not the rapacious commanders had so much trouble finding space to store their booty that open carts groaning under the wealth of the Indies could have been seen trundling through the streets in open daylight? Parliament was in session at this very time for the purpose of finding money to keep England herself afloat.

How then could His Lordship have taken it upon himself to enrich himself out of His Majesty's prizes? Every man, almost it seemed, turned against the Earl of Sandwich. Mr. Pepys would do whatever was necessary to disengage himself from the thorny business and, for that matter, in the months ahead to disengage himself from His Lordship. On October 28, 1665, Mr. Pepys referred to His Lordship's "disgrace" in the matter of the prize goods. An order had come from Court countermanding the Duke of Albemarle's order entrusting the goods to the East India Company and to have them delivered to the sub-commissioners of prizes. Mr. Pepys assumed that His Majesty would take the proper steps to relieve his faithful subject His Lordship, Edward Montagu, Earl of Sandwich, who had contrived and actually restored him to the throne of England, from the heavy pressures that would surely result in his downfall.

By the end of October, 1665, Pepys reported that he had heard that the number dying of The Plague was four hundred, but that the number dead from the disease was 1,031. He complained of the sad times and his own problems: lack of money in the navy put everything out of order; men grew mutinous; and nobody minded the business of the navy but himself. There was comfort, nevertheless, for optimistic Mr. Pepys in the thought that his new job as Surveyor General of the Victualling carried an additional annual salary of £300, and that this stipend would be just a token of the gratuities that he would get from merchants, factors, chapmen, and slopsellers to His Majesty's Navy. He was prospering even in this time of pestilence.

V Mr. Pepys Resumes Life in the City

When Mr. Pepys visited London on November 24, there was a decided lifting of the gloom that had hung over the city. Men and women were bustling about; the shopkeepers were taking down the shutters; and the merchants were on the Exchange. Mr. Pepys, a man who loved to celebrate auspicious occasions, stopped at the old oyster shop in Gracious Street and, always with an eye for fishwives, "bought two barrels of my fine woman of the shop." He was pleased to observe that she was alive after The Plague, and he stated that everybody enquired about the fate of everybody he knew. It was as though he had been afraid to ask about Mr. Goodman So-and-So or this man or that man, fearing to have learned that The Plague had taken him away; but today he felt like asking, because he had the reasonable assurance that the answer would be that that friend or neighbor had been spared. He was glad to see the Exchange so full of people, and expressed hopes for an abatement in the Mortality Bill next week.

With the waning of The Plague, men's confidence returned, and many who had sought safety in the suburbs of London and in the nearby towns and villages returned to the city. On December 4, Mr. Pepys reported that he had kept open the office at his London lodgings, going home to dinner that his wife had prepared for him. "And it was a joyful thing for us to meet here," he admits, "for which God be praised." An important revelation of the *Diary* is that even in times of catastrophe men must come to terms with life and its petty daily concerns.

When Mr. and Mrs. Pepys returned home to their London lodgings on Sunday, January 7, 1666, and let the air course through the house, they decided that the bedroom looked tired and that it would be a good idea to spend a little money freshening it. And after supper, Mr. Pepys reports, "with great joy in my heart for my coming once again hither, to bed." These homely but symbolic acts tell that The Plague had run its course. No man knew this better than Pepys, who, although spared, had been close to death in the daily round.

CHAPTER 11

The Great Fire

DISASTER though it was, the fire fumigated The Plague clean out of London town. At first, when Jane awakened Pepys before dawn on the morning of September 2, 1666, to tell him of a fire raging in the distance, Mr. Pepys thought so little of the danger that he went back to sleep. His account of the fire of September 2 to 6 is one of the greatest reports of "what happened" in the annals of man. By and by the maid came back into the room to tell him that she had heard that over three hundred houses had burned down during the night and that the fire was now destroying the buildings on Fish Street by London Bridge. Mr. Pepys got ready to go see for himself.

When he reached the Tower of London, he climbed to one of the high places and Sir J. Robinson's little son went with him. The spectacular elements of the great blaze impressed Pepys, but he thought immediately of his favorite Betty Michell who dwelt in the path of the fire. Seeking an official person, the lieutenant of the Tower, he learned from him that the fire had started in the King's baker's house in Pudding Lane and that it had already burned St. Magnus's Church and, as Jane had reported, most of Fish Street. Going down to the waterside for a closer perspective, he hired a boat and stood off from shore, noting that the fire had consumed Mr. Michell's house and all in its path as far as the Old Swan; and, while he stood there, it reached as far as the Steel Yard.

People acted as expected, trying to remove their goods; they were flinging things into the river or into any boat that lay offshore; others, in fact, were clinging to house and goods until the very fire touched them; and some leaped from house to house by way of the waterside staircases. Pepys noticed, too, that the frightened pigeons clung to perches and dovecotes until their wings caught the flames and they fell to the fiery street. Before his very eyes, his schoolmate Elborough's church caught fire in its steeple, which then toppled to the ground; all things seemed combustible, even the very stones of the churches, after the long summer drought.

I *Mr. Pepys Is Appointed Fire Marshall*

People stood riveted in horror or ran aimlessly about, but none did a thing to stop the conflagration. Hiring a boat, Mr. Pepys went directly to Whitehall. At Whitehall he went directly to the King's private chapel, and a group of excited persons gathered around him for news of the fire. Word that he was there was taken to the King who gave him a royal audience and an opportunity to make a vitally sensible suggestion: "So I was called for, and did tell the King and Duke of York what I saw and that unless his Majesty did command houses to be pulled down nothing could stop the fire . . . and the King commanded me to go to my Lord Mayor from him and command him to spare no houses, but to pull down before the fire every way. . . ." The Duke of York offered that the Lord Mayor could have as many soldiers as he wished to carry out the order.

With this splendid sense of combining official with personal accounts, and large circumstance with little, Mr. Pepys reported that he met Captain Cocke, borrowed his coach, picked up John Creed, and sped off to St. Paul's. From there he walked as best he could along Watling Street, catching a quick glance at the "extraordinary good goods carried in carts and on backs," and at people bearing away the sick in their beds. When he found the Lord Mayor and gave him the King's command, the response was that of "a fainting woman"; but the poor man had already done what he could and, indeed, had been pulling down houses only to be overtaken by the leaping flames. Reaching the human breaking point, he told Mr. Pepys that he needed more soldiers, that he had been fire-fighting all night, and that he needed to refresh himself. And so the two officials parted, leaving the fire to run awhile.

Quite understandably, after evidence of such ineptness in the one man really responsible to play the Chief Fire Marshall's part, Mr. Pepys turned homeward to Seething Lane; but he took the circuitous route. As he walked, he noticed that the close-built houses were full of combustible materials such as the pitch and tar in Thames Street and that the warehouses contained oil, wine, brandy, and other redolent things. He met handsome Isaac Houblon, "prettily dressed and dirty," at his door at Dowgate, receiving some of his brother's goods; and Mr. Houblon told him that the goods had been removed twice already. When Mr. Pepys got home, past noon, he found guests who had come to see his fine closet: "Mr. Wood and his wife Barbary Sheldon, and also Mr. Moore: she mighty fine, and her husband, for aught I see, a likely man."

II *Mr. Pepys Saves His Belongings*

This was no time to pamper Mr. Pepys's vanities, and he admitted being in great trouble and disturbance, not knowing what to think of the disaster. The following statement can only be explained by stating that it comes from inexplicable, irrepressible Mr. Samuel Pepys: "However, we had an extraordinary good dinner, and as merry as at this time we could be." As soon as dinner was over, Mr. Pepys and Mr. Moore[1] left the house to take another look at the fire—to take inventory, as it were, noticing the thronged streets with people and carts and horses jostled together, and removing goods from a burned house to an as yet untouched one. Mr. Pepys flitted up and down the city; and, although he was obviously frightened, he blazed with excitement and he enjoyed the holocaust with the wonder of a little boy.

But his impersonal wonder and excitement gave way at last to grave thoughts and to the upward rush of sympathetic sensibilities: "we saw the fire as only one entire arch of fire from this to the other side of the bridge, and in a bow up the hill for an arch of above a mile long: it made me weep to see it. The churches, houses, and all one fire and flaming at once; and a horrid noise the flames made, and the cracking of houses at their ruine. So home with a sad heart, and there find every body discoursing and lamenting the fire; and poor Tom Hater[2] come with some few of his goods saved out of his house, which is burned upon Fish-streete Hill." Offering him asylum from the flames, Mr. Pepys received Mr. Hayter and his goods; but it were as though he had brought the flames to Seething Lane since the Pepys household was compelled to pack its own goods and to carry them by moonlight into the garden. With Tom Hayter's help, Mr. Pepys carried silver and iron chests into the

cellar, but he kept his bags of gold and precious papers in order
to carry them away.

On the morning of September 4, the fire still raced through
the narrow London streets, but by that time Mr. Pepys had
carted his essential possessions to Sir William Rider's place at
Bethnal Green, and he could indulge the pleasure of deciding
what to do with certain luxuries and less momentous papers. He
and Sir William Penn dug a pit in the garden to store their wine
and Mr. Pepys's precious Parmesan cheese. With mounting fury
the fire raced in and out of the streets and corners of the old
city, burst in and out of doors, and leaped across the narrow
alleys, hiding in the rafters and licking at the cornices. Before
two o'clock on the morning of September 5, the fire had reached
Barking Church at the bottom of Seething Lane, and Mr. Pepys
decided quickly to carry his gold and Mrs. Pepys away. He had
two thousand three hundred and fifty pounds in his house. In
Proundy's boat, going to Woolwich, he and Mrs. Pepys, Jane, and
Will Hewer saw the whole city on fire; and as far as Woolwich
the fire stayed with them.

III *Master of Exquisite Details*

When he returned from Woolwich, Mr. Pepys felt certain that
by this time the navy office and his living quarters in Seething
Lane had surrendered to the flames. He was happily surprised
to find that, by the razing of houses and with the great help
given by the workmen out of the King's yards, a "good stop" had
been given the fire: "it having only burned the dyall of Barking
Church, and part of the porch, and was there quenched."

Following a natural impulse to get a panoramic view of the
desolation, Mr. Pepys climbed to the top of Barking Church
steeple. And from there he saw "the saddest sight of desolation
. . . every where great fires, oyle cellars, and brimstone. . . ."
Overcome with fright, he sought firm ground: "and I walked into
the town, and find Fanchurch-Streete, and Gracious-Streete, and
Lumbard-Streete all in dust. The Exchange a sad sight, nothing
standing there, of all the statues or pillars, but Sir Thomas
Gresham's picture in the corner. . . ."

So hot was the going that Mr. Pepys cried out that his "feet
were ready to burn, walking through the towne among the hot
coles." He complained, too, though not harshly, of the profiteer,

always present in disaster; for Mr. Pepys "paid twopence for a plain penny loaf." And he saw such unforgettable sights as "a poor cat taken out of a hole in the chimney, joyning to the wall of the Exchange, with the hair all burned off the body, and yet alive." On September 6, he reported the cleaning women scolding for drinks and some already drunk as devils; and then he added: "I saw good butts of sugar broke open in the street, and people go and take handsfull out, and put into beer, and drink it."

On September 7 Mr. Pepys indicated that the fire had been brought under control, and that the London authorities had taken some practical steps to relieve the suffering: the churches were to be opened to receive poor people, markets were to be kept at Leadenhall and Mile-end-green, and a new and vigorous city was to rise from the ashes of the old. Those whose homes were left standing would accommodate for the time being friends and neighbors; and Mr. Pepys, who had torn everything down and moved everything from his lodgings, would find a bed at his neighbor's, Sir William Penn's. There he slept in his drawers, bereft of bed clothes; but his sleep was fitful, since he was frightened of new outbreaks of fire. At the slightest suspicion thereafter of a fire, Mr. Pepys almost died of fright.

Conclusion

WHEN the *Diary* closed in 1669, Mr. Pepys was a substantial, successful man. Troubled with poor eyesight, tired from the press of business, and attempting to pacify his wife, when she came upon him "suddenly . . . embracing the girl con [his] hand sub su coats . . . ," on the evening of October 25, 1668, he decided to take a vacation on the Continent. After taking considerable time to put personal and public affairs in shape, he petitioned the Duke of York and received his permission on May 19, 1669, "to go into Holland to observe things there." His Majesty graciously consented, and the Duke advised Mr. Pepys to pretend he was going "into the country somewhere," probably to prevent jealousy among his colleagues.

Always a man to mix a little business with pleasures, he made observations and collections of notes respecting the French and Dutch navies and had a generally pleasant and profitable journey. Soon after his return to England, his wife became ill of a fever and died on November 10, 1669, in the twenty-ninth year of her life and in the fourteenth of her lively marriage. She was buried in St. Olave's, where Mr. Pepys erected an imposing monument to her memory.

I *The Later Years*

His parliamentary ambition prompted Mr. Pepys to seek the seat for Aldborough, Suffolk, that had been made vacant by the death of Sir Robert Brooke; but, despite the active support of the Duke of York and Lord Henry Howard, Mr. Pepys failed of election, no doubt, in part because his wife's illness and death prevented active electioneering.

Gratitude was ever one of Mr. Pepys's virtues; and, even if His Lordship had become a liability to him in the later years, the Clerk of the Acts must have been deeply sorrowful at the loss of one who had done so many tangible turns to help him out of the doldrums of pen and paper. His Lordship, patron and kinsman Sir Edward Montagu, Earl of Sandwich, Vice-Admiral of the Fleet, perished with his flagship the *Royal James* in a naval battle with the Dutch on May 28, 1672, beset by gout and the loss of fortune and reputation. His body was recovered and given a hero's burial in Westminster Abbey with the rising Clerk of the Acts, Samuel Pepys, attending among the noble mourners.

If substantial successes lay ahead for Mr. Pepys, there were also serious political troubles; for Mr. Pepys was caught in the plots and sub-plots that vexed England when it became evident that Charles would sire no legitimate heir to the throne and that Catholic James was the heir-presumptive. Some vague statements made by the Earl of Shaftesbury and Sir John Banks that Mr. Pepys kept a crucifix or a picture of the crucifixion in his house caused Mr. Pepys to be accused of being a Catholic or of having secret Catholic ties. He did indeed have such a memento, among scores of others, in his house; for he mentions Lovett's varnishing his "fine Crucifix" in the *Diary* (July 20, 1666), as well as the "print of the passion" that Lovett had delivered, framed and varnished, on November 3. In any event, charges could not be supported on such evidence; Shaftesbury and Banks could not sustain them; and the accusation was dropped.

His intimate connections with James, Duke of York, made Mr. Pepys a rather obvious and vulnerable target during the so-called Popish Plot; and his clerk Samuel Atkins was among those accused of being accessory to the murder of Sir Edmund Berry Godfrey, a sensational political murder mystery. Sir Edmund Berry Godfrey, a Justice of the Peace and dealer in firewood, had once incurred King Charles's disfavor for having arrested one of the King's physicians, Sir Alexander Frazier, for non-payment of a bill. Mr. Pepys recorded the incident and some of its political consequences in the *Diary* on May 26, 1669. It is necessary to oversimplify accounts of the circumstances of Godfrey's murder and merely to agree with one of Mr. Pepys's biographers, Sir Arthur Bryant, that it was lucky for Mr. Pepys that His Majesty had summoned him to Newmarket on Friday, October 11, 1678, and that he was with the King when Sir Edmund's body was discovered. Mr. Pepys could not be connected with the murder in any way, but anti-Catholic feelings were running high and Mr. Pepys had become closely identified with the King's brother, Catholic James, Duke of York.

Protestant wrath spilled over on Mr. Pepys, who was accused by one Colonel John Scott of having sent, in 1675, information concerning the English navy to the French and of plotting to overthrow Protestantism in England. If the *Diary* had been available, no sane man reading it could have given credence to either charge; for Mr. Pepys had written his Protestantism into the *Diary* and had built himself into the fabric of the navy. Mr.

Pepys was committed to the Tower on May 22, 1679, and his clerk Thomas Hayter succeeded him at the navy office.

Scott's charges put Mr. Pepys to the trouble and expense of finding evidence to attack his credibility. Mr. Pepys appointed his brother-in-law Balthasar St. Michel to seek such evidence, especially in France where "Balty," now a considerable naval person in his own right, had connections by birth and persuasion. He was not sparing in his expense account, but facts that he unearthed, several legal postponements, and Scott's refusal to support the charges brought about Mr. Pepys's release. His name seemed entirely cleared when in March, 1680, his butler John James confessed on his deathbed that he had been bribed by William Harboard, M. P., an enemy of Mr. Pepys, to make the pro-Catholic charges.

The easy-going, safe days of the navy meetings and his lodgings in Seething Lane had passed away, and Mr. Pepys was out of public office until 1684 when he was appointed Secretary of the Admiralty with an annual salary of five hundred pounds. Honors and responsibilities were placed upon him in and out of public office, and he remained in close association regarding navy matters with Charles until the end of his reign in 1685 and with James, who succeeded to the throne, until the end of his reign in 1688.

Among the honors that came to Mr. Pepys in his later years were elections to Master of the Trinity House in 1676 and Master of the Clothworkers Company in 1677. He was chosen to represent Harwich and sat as its representative in the Short Parliament of 1679, and he again represented the borough in 1685. In 1682, he accompanied the Duke of York to Scotland; in 1683, Pepys was on the Commission to Tangier and went with Lord Dartmouth to dismantle the works and garrison at that outpost of empire. He also wrote a diary of this expedition; but, excepting an occasional sparkle, the brilliant spontaneity of the style of the *Diary* had gone. The Presidency of the Royal Society was bestowed upon him in 1684 and he participated, this time as more than an interloper, in the coronation of James, Duke of York, in 1685; he marched in the procession as a Baron of the Cinque Ports.

At the rumored elevation to the peerage in 1673 of Sir Robert Paston, member of Parliament for Castle Rising, Mr. Pepys sought the Duke of York's aid and that of Lord Henry Howard, resident and landlord, to be chosen to fill the Parliamentary vacancy. The local burghers objected to absentee representation, the seat was contested, and the Parliamentary Committee on Privileges declared the seat vacant. Anti-Catholicism was vocal, and Mr. Pepys's close connections with Catholic James and, now, with Catholic Lord Howard made him unpopular with his would-be constituency. After some difficulties with his unscrupulous opponent Robert Offley, Mr. Pepys assumed his place as member of Parliament. This victory, nevertheless, earned the ill-will of Lord Shaftesbury, leader of the anti-Catholic partisans.

When James was deposed in 1688, Mr. Pepys lost his office of Secretary of the Admiralty to Phineas Bowles; and on June 25, 1689, he was committed to the Gatehouse on charges of having given naval information to the French. He spent the remainder of his years in retirement at Clapham with his former clerk, body-guard, and now devoted friend, Will Hewer. Still active and inquisitive, the elder statesman devoted himself to correspondence and good works. His collected letters, in charming if somewhat stiff epistolary style, include those to Sir Isaac Newton; Sir Christopher Wren; admirable friend and fellow diarist John Evelyn; members of his and Paulina Pepys Jackson's family; and a host of men famous enough in their day, if not in ours. These letters show Mr. Pepys the same mettlesome, generous, shrewd man that he always was and remained to the end.

When he died in Clapham on May 26, 1703, an autopsy revealed large kidney stones. To the poor and to servants Pepys left generous gifts. The funeral arrangements included the sending of rings and mourning cloth to officials, friends, relatives, and godsiblings in all stations of life; the recipients included reverend clergy, lords, schoolmen, surgeons and apothecaries, bookbinders, lawyers, lesser men, and Mrs. Mary Skinner, who sometimes presided over his household. John Evelyn, invited to be a pallbearer, but, infirm with age, could not attend; but he wrote a gracious elegy to Pepys in his own *Diary*. The funeral procession went to St. Olave's Church were Mr. Samuel Pepys was buried on the night of June 4, 1703.

II *The Diarist*

The *Diary* brings us into intimate contact with one of the most remarkable men who ever lived and, yet, a truly average man with typical faults as well as virtues. To use a good, if overworked, phrase, Mr. Pepys was the "divine average"; for, in many ways, he was the best of men. When death lurked and danger threatened, he did not run and hide; he stood his ground —in plague and fire and war, and he watched in open-mouthed wonder. He did, though, what average man has done since time began: he took part in things. There were crises in Pepys's day as in ours. Average men today, and always, will face fire and flood, pestilence and deprivation with quiet determination as did Pepys.

The paradox of the *Diary* is that average days to average men are not ordinary at all, for they assume a vast importance to each man. There is no evidence anywhere in the *Diary* that Pepys thought of himself as special or as remarkable in any way. Vain and self-conscious he was, indeed, and lovably and delightfully so; but the sin of pride—of vainglory—was not a sin of Samuel Pepys. The average man who reads the *Diary* may be pleased to recognize himself in Mr. Pepys. When Mr. Pepys viewed the Coronation, he stationed a comely woman next to Mrs. Pepys so that from a distance he could watch her decently; when pestilence came, he rubbed himself with plug tobacco as any man might do to ward off evil by reaching into the dark, backward abyss of time to invoke a charm or to practice a forgotten rite; but Pepys stayed among the comfortless and dying; when fire broke out, Pepys ran to see it but stayed to put it out. These great events happened on average days, for any day is an average day; but Mr. Pepys threaded the events together by taking part in them. The secret of the power of Mr. Pepys and his *Diary* is that Mr. Pepys shows average man that, while doing average things, if he take his part in the daily round, his days, too, are filled with meaning and living wonder.

The literary quality of the *Diary* depends, to a large extent, on its simplicity of style and on the personal grace revealed in Mr. Pepys's way with words. He wrote down what he witnessed and shared of the life about him while the incidents were fresh in his mind. There may be a slight hint here and there in the *Diary* that Mr. Pepys wished some day to edit it for print but it is, in fact, a spontaneous record of things as they happened from day to day. Mr. Pepys's friend and contemporary, John Evelyn, wrote a wonderful diary, too, and always it invites comparison with Pepys's; neither suffers from the comparison. Evelyn's diary represents the edited and thrice-pondered account; Pepys's represents things as they happened, on the spot.

Notes and References

Chapter One

1. *The Diary of Samuel Pepys* (New York, London, n.d.), September 2, 1666.
2. *Ibid.*, April 23, 1661.

Chapter Two

1. The part of the Long Parliament remaining after the purge of 1648 until Oliver Cromwell disbanded it in 1653; the same body was recalled in 1659 and disbanded in 1660.
2. John Lambert (1619-1683?) was major-general in the parliamentary army.
3. George Monk (1608-1676), also spelled Monck, parliamentary general, aided Charles's restoration to the throne in 1660, and was created Knight of the Garter and Duke of Albemarle by him.
4. *Diary*, June 23, 1665.
5. The Michells, frequently mentioned in the *Diary*, were booksellers at Westminster Hall.
6. Probably the wife of sea-going Captain Murford, frequently mentioned in the *Diary*.
7. His Lordship was appointed to this sinecure in early June, 1660.
8. *Diary*, March 9, 1669.
9. Edward Pickering, brother of Sir Gilbert Pickering, was a man-about-town; frequently mentioned in derogatory fashion in the *Diary*.
10. Dr. Clarke was a member of the Royal Society and was appointed a physician in ordinary to Charles II in 1667.
11. Sir Edward Hyde, first Earl of Clarendon, had been entrusted with the Great Seal and the title Lord Chancellor by Charles in 1658, before the Restoration. His daughter Ann married James, Duke of York, in September, 1660.
12. Thomas Wriothesley, Earl of Southampton, 1607-1667.
13. Thomas Povy, a substantial property man and office-holder, was Treasurer and Receiver-General of the Rents and Revenues for James, Duke of York, until 1668. Mr. Pepys mentions him in the *Diary* in many connections, including his elegance as host and householder, but he was a poor manager and execrable accountant whom Mr. Pepys succeeded as Treasurer for Tangier on March 20, 1665.
14. John Creed appears constantly in the *Diary*. Pepys often refers to him slightingly, and he seems to have been of humble birth. He filled several minor positions under Charles II and married Elizabeth Pickering, daughter of Sir Gilbert Pickering, Bart., and niece of Sir Edward Montagu, First Earl of Sandwich, his and Mr. Pepys's patron.
15. Appointed Commissioner of the Navy in May, 1662, Mr. Coventry (later Sir William), Privy Councillor, was a friend and favorite of Mr. Pepys, sometime Secretary to the Duke of York, and a very able man. He lost the King's favor and was temporarily sent to the Tower.
16. William Hewer was Mr. Pepys's clerk and gradually came to be his

Notes and References

friend. He was the nephew of Robert Blackburne, former Secretary of the Admiralty, and as a seventeen-year-old hireling was somewhat erratic at first while serving his master at the office, at home, and as frequent attendant and companion (Arthur Bryant, *Samuel Pepys*, I, 118). He was appointed Deputy Judge Advocate of the Fleet in 1677, Commissioner of the Navy in 1685, was elected M. P. for Yarmouth, Isle of Wright, in 1685. He also served as Treasurer for Tangier. Mr. Pepys died in his house at Clapham, previously owned by Sir Dennis Gauden (Henry B. Wheatley, ed. *The Diary of Samuel Pepys*, I, 137n).

17. A page of the King's bedchamber and Keeper of his private closet.

18. Betty Lane, later Mrs. Martin, a seamstress and haberdasher at Westminster Hall, was an intimate of Mr. Pepys; she maintained their relationship even after marrying Mr. Martin.

Chapter Three

1. Will and Anthony Joyce, brothers, were married to Katherine and Mary Fenner, daughters of Thomas Fenner, Mr. Pepys's mother's brother-in-law. In the *Diary*, Mr. Pepys refers to in-laws as though they were blood relations.

2. Anthony Ashley Cooper, created Baron Ashley in 1661, and Earl of Shaftesbury, 1672, is believed to be an object of Dryden's famous anti-Whig satire "Absolom and Achitophel."

Chapter Four

1. Mrs. Knepp was one of his favorite ladies and allowed Mr. Pepys many liberties; he described her husband as "an ill, melancholy, jealous-looking fellow. . . ." (*Diary*, December 8, 1665).

Chapter Five

1. Captain Cooke was Choirmaster of the Children of the Chapel Royal.

2. Mrs. Bagwell was a special intimate of Mr. Pepys who carried on a rather disreputable affair with her, sometimes with her husband perilously close by.

3. Sir Hugh Cholmely, member of the Tangier Commission, later became Governor of Tangier.

4. Henry Killigrew was the son of playwright and court jester, Thomas Killigrew.

5. She was the daughter of John Pepys of South Creake and wife of Sergeant John Turner.

6. The *Diary* refers to her as "a pretty wench"; she married Mr. Markham, a kinsman of Sir William Penn (*Diary*, August 5, 1666).

Chapter Six

1. Sir John Denham wrote the famous descriptive poem "Cooper's Hill."

2. William Howe appears often in the *Diary*; although Mr. Pepys criticizes him and he was sometimes in trouble, they were good friends. He was appointed Deputy Treasurer of the Navy, September 18, 1665.

Chapter Seven

1. Mr. Pepys received a Latin diploma from Oxford University in 1701 for commissioning the painter Sir Godfrey Kneller to paint a portrait of Mr. John Wallis, Savilian Professor of Geometry at Oxford.

2. Mr. Pepys succeeded Sir Cyril Wyche as President of the Royal Society in 1684.

3. Mr. Pepys was chosen Master of Trinity House in 1676 and, again, in 1685.

Chapter Eight

1. Dr. James Pierce was Surgeon to the Duke of York; the Pierces are mentioned frequently in the *Diary*.

2. The Colemans were musical and dancing friends of Mr. Pepys.

3. John Evelyn and Mr. Pepys were friends, enjoying many contacts. Evelyn's diary covers a long span from 1640 to 1706, the year of his death. His diary, not so personal and human as Mr. Pepys's, is in the nature of an edited journal of events.

Chapter Nine

1. Thomas Killigrew, a long-time favorite and attendant of King Charles, was an outstanding playwright.

2. Captain William Ferrers, frequently mentioned in the *Diary*, was the Earl of Sandwich's master of horse.

3. Lady Castlemaine, the wife of Roger Palmer, created Earl of Castlemaine in 1661, is generally recognized as King Charles's favorite mistress, exercising considerable political influence at court. Among the titles that His Majesty conferred upon her were Baroness Nonsuch, Countess of Southampton, and Duchess of Cleveland. She is said to have borne him six children.

4. Dryden's use of the heroic couplet in writing heroic plays set off a sharp controversy with his playwriting brother-in-law, Sir Robert Howard, whose positive views on all matters occasioned Shadwell's lampooning him as Sir Positive-at-all in the play *The Impertinents*.

5. Thomas Shadwell, author of *The Impertinents*, suffers from the reputation of being "prince of dullness," fastened on him by Dryden in the poem "Macflecknoe" as a result of the bitter controversy over the succession to Charles's throne. Actually, Shadwell's plays are quite as well written as the average Restoration play.

Chapter Ten

1. Captain George Cocke, merchant, held several minor jobs during the Restoration; for example, steward for sick and wounded seamen, and had many business transactions with Mr. Pepys, including the disputed prize goods.

Chapter Eleven

1. Mr. Moore appears frequently in the *Diary* and enjoyed Mr. Pepys's friendship; he was connected with the Earl of Sandwich, although the connection is not clear.

2. Thomas Hayter was Pepys's clerk at the navy office; he was appointed Clerk of the Acts in 1674 and Secretary of the Admiralty in 1679.

Selected Bibliography

Primary Sources

CHAPWELL, EDWIN. (Transcriber and Editor). *Shorthand Letters of Samuel Pepys.* Cambridge: The University Press, 1933. The letters are addressed to the Earl of Sandwich, Mr. (later Sir) William Coventry, Colonel Middleton, and other official persons. Although written in formal seventeenth-century epistolary style, the prose of the letters matches that of the *Diary* in vigorous style.

HOWARTH, R. G. Editor. *Letters and the Second Diary of Samuel Pepys.* London and Toronto: J. M. Dent and Sons, Ltd.; New York: E. P. Dutton and Co., Inc., 1932. Although interesting and concise, Pepys's letters seem to have lost some of the zest of earlier ones. This second *Diary*, though factual, is generally dull. It is a record of his journey to Tangier in 1683, his travels in Spain, and the return journey in 1684.

KENYON, J. P. Editor. *Samuel Pepys's Diary* (abridged). New York: Macmillan Company, 1963. A useful, if abridged, edition of the *Diary* with essential entries.

TANNER, JOSEPH ROBSON. Editor. *Private Correspondence and Miscellaneous Papers of Samuel Pepys, 1679-1703.* London: G. Bell and Sons, Ltd., 1926, 2 vols. This miscellany provides important information on Pepys's busy, complex life.

WHEATLEY, HENRY B. Editor. *The Diary of Samuel Pepys.* New York: Random House (by arrangement with Messrs. G. Bell and Sons, Ltd., 1893). There are several good editions of the *Diary*: the original, transscribed in 1825; Lord Braybrook's in several editions; the Reverend Mynors Bright's, and others; but all have omissions for a variety of reasons, including modesty or squeamishness. Omissions of entries in the Wheatley edition: November 26, 1661; March 25 and May 13, 1662, and August 30, 1663, are unexplained. The editor observes the amenities in suspension points, but he does not attempt to conceal the diarist's occasional misconduct. Impressive bibliographical material, an exhaustive index, and good print make the Wheatley edition of the *Diary* a delight for the reader.

Secondary Sources

ABERNETHY, CECIL. *Mr. Pepys of Seething Lane.* New York: McGraw-Hill Book Company, Inc., 1957. A well-written book, based primarily upon the *Diary*. It re-creates Mr. Pepys's contacts, especially with persons who frequented the navy office in Seething Lane.

BRADFORD, GAMALIEL. *The Soul of Samuel Pepys.* Boston and New York: Houghton Mifflin Company, 1924. A biographical account and an appreciation based on the *Diary*.

BRIDGE, SIR FREDERICK. *Samuel Pepys Lover of Music.* London: Smith, Elder and Company, 1903. The author, King Edward Professor of Music in the University of London, writes authoritatively on amateur musician Pepys in a carefully written, appreciative book.

BRYANT, SIR ARTHUR. *Samuel Pepys the Man in the Making.* London: Collins, 1933. An impressively documented account of the early years supported by accounts in the *Diary.*

————. *Samuel Pepys the Years of Peril.* London: Collins, 1935. This is the second volume of the biography; evenly matched in quality with the first, it details Pepys's increasing involvement in Restoration politics.

————. *Samuel Pepys the Saviour of the Navy.* London: Collins, 1938. The third volume completes the biography and serves as a model for a well-balanced judicious account of Pepys's services to his country.

COHEN, SELMA JEANNE. "Mr. Pepys Learns to Dance," *Dance Magazine,* XXX (March, 1956), 36. An account of Pepys's efforts to learn and practice social dancing.

DALE, D. "Greatness of Samuel Pepys," *Quarterly Review,* 275 (October, 1940), 227-38. An appreciation of Pepys, based mainly on the *Diary.*

————. "Mutilation of Pepys's *Diary,*" *London Quarterly and Holborn Review,* 166 (April, 1941), 219-20. A discussion of the condition of the text and textual problems.

EDEN, CECIL S. *Pepys Himself.* London: Oxford University Press, 1963. This little book (143 pages) is, basically, a fine character study of Pepys. Based primarily on the *Diary,* it uses a minimum of biographical details.

HUNT, PERCIVAL. *Samuel Pepys in the Diary.* Pittsburgh: the University Press, 1958. A charming book based on the *Diary;* shows sharp insights into Mr. Pepys's character and his dealings with his contemporaries.

LUCAS-DUBRETON, J. *Samuel Pepys A Portrait in Miniature.* New York and London: G. P. Putnam's Sons, 1925. Fictionalized biography based on the *Diary;* gives a topical account of Pepys's activities.

MCAFEE, HELEN. *Pepys on the Restoration Stage.* New Haven: Yale University Press, 1916. Based on Pepys's record in the *Diary* of his theater activities; a comprehensive study of plays, actors, audiences, theaters, etc., of the Restoration era.

PONSONBY, ARTHUR. *Samuel Pepys.* London: Macmillan Company, 1928. Deals with Pepys and his contemporaries, notably his friend, the famous diarist John Evelyn. The author, a distinguished scholar of diaries and diary writing, based his study on the *Diary.*

POWER, SIR D'ARCY. "Why Samuel Pepys Discontinued His *Diary.*" *Selected Writings 1877-1930.* Oxford: The Clarendon Press, 1931. An amusing, if scientific, account of psychosomatic, hypochondriac Samuel Pepys, who suffered, among other maladies, from "hypermetropic astigmatism."

RANFT, B. M. "Significance of the Political Career of Samuel Pepys," *Journal of Modern History,* XXIV (December, 1952), 368-75. Compactly written account of Mr. Pepys's political activities in relation to his times.

TANNER, JOSEPH ROBSON. "Pepys and the Popish Plot," *English Historical Review,* VII, no. 26, (April, 1892), 281-90. Study of Pepys's difficulties with his so-called Catholic sympathies.

Selected Bibliography

TURNER, D. C. *Samuel Pepys Esquire Secretary of the Admiralty to King Charles and King James the Second.* (A pamphlet, 18 pp.) Cambridge: University Press, n.d. A valuable account of the Pepys Library at Magdalene College, Cambridge. Describes the Pepys bequests and their history, the medieval manuscripts, early printed books and other incunabula, the special collections, prints and ballads, and books intimately connected with Pepys's life. This valuable brochure is embellished with a pen-sketch of its title showing a peacock and flying birds with the letters Samuel Pepys ornately adorned. The back of this pamphlet bears a reproduction of Pepys's coat-of-arms: the inscription at the top is *mens cujusque is est Quisque* on a curled riband above crossed sea-anchors with S P wrapping their shafts and a navy-rope gracefully intertwining the whole design. Distributed at the Pepys Library, the brochure contains excellent pictures and portraits, including a mature, stern Pepys by Kneller, *aet. c.* 54.

WEISS, DAVID S. *Samuel Pepys Curiosa.* Pittsburgh: The University Press, 1957. Skillfully written book, based primarily on the *Diary*, deals with Pepys's versatility and preoccupation with music.

WHEATLEY, HENRY B. *Samuel Pepys and the World He Lived In.* 5th ed. London: S. Sonnenchein, 1907. Fascinating account of the England of Pepys's day, its people, customs.

Index

Adventures of Five Hours, The, 115

Albemarle, Duke of (George Monk, formerly General of the Army), 17, 19, 24, 37, 41, 42, 88, 90, 138

Alchemist, The, 17, 24, 39, 41, 42, 88, 90, 121, 138, 140

Andrews, Jr., 59, 60, 104

Argalus and Parthenia, 130

Ashwell, Mary, 71, 72, 73, 74, 111

Aynsworth, Mrs., 93, 94

Bacon, Sir Francis, 98

Bagwell, William, 84, 85

Bagwell, Mrs., 66, 82, 84, 85, 137

Barons of the Cinque Ports, 19, 149

Bartholomew Fair, 118, 121, 122

Batten, Sir William, Navy Commissioner, 23, 29-31, 33, 35, 36, 44, 45, 66, 88, 135, 138

Beaumont, Francis, and Fletcher, John, 113, 114, 123-27, 129, 130, 131

Beggar's Bush, 129

"Bell" tavern, 85

Bence, Alderman, 137

Betterton, Thomas, 113, 118, 124, 125

Betterton, Mrs., 125, 126

Black Prince, The, 128

Blagrave, Thomas, 101, 107, 108

Bondman, The, 113, 124

Book of Common Prayer, The, 20, 89

Boyle, Dr., 40, 96

Brampton, 16, 46, 62, 68, 69, 73, 74, 78, 93, 94, 95

Bristol, Earl of, 125

Brooke, Sir Robert, 147

Brouncker, William, Viscount, 30, 35, 40, 43-45, 47, 53, 96, 138, 139

"Bull Head" tavern, 46

Bunyan, John, 19, 22

Burnett, Dr. Alexander, 19, 133

Bussy d'Ambois, 114

Butler, Samuel, 100

Calamy, Edmund, The Reverend, 81

Calvin, John, 76

Cambridge University, 92-94, 96, 97, 99, 116

Canterbury, Archbishop of, 40

Cardinal, The, 114

Carlell, Ludovic, 116, 123, 127, 131

Carteret, Sir George, 24, 31, 35-37, 40, 45, 57, 58, 66, 88, 134, 135, 136

Carteret, Philip, 24, 134, 135

Castlemaine, Lady (Mrs. Palmer), 84, 114, 115, 126, 127

Castle Rising, 37

Catiline, 122, 131

Changes, The, or Love in a Maze, 123, 125

Chapman, George, 114

Charles I, 34, 132

Charles, Prince (later Charles II), 17, 19, 22, 24, 26, 31, 32, 34, 37, 38, 40, 41-44, 46, 48, 50, 61, 62, 81, 84, 86, 88-91, 95,

101, 114-16, 119, 125-27, 134, 139, 140, 143, 147, 148, 149

Chaucer, 19, 22, 100, 102

Christ's College, Cambridge, 92, 93

Claracilla, 115

Clarendon, Edward Hyde, Earl of, 32, 34, 36, 37, 39, 40, 127

Clarges, Sir Thomas, 27, 100, 102

Clarke, Dr. Timothy, 35, 40, 96, 114

Cocke, Captain George, 104, 137-39, 143

Coffee House, The, 128

Coleman, Edward, 103, 104

Colet, Dean, 98

College of Virtuosos, The (The Royal Society), 18

Committee, The, 126

Corneille, 116, 122, 127

Cornwallis, Lord, 89

Coronation of Charles II, 19, 88, 151

Country Captain, The, 113

Coventry, Sir William, 27, 31-33, 35, 37, 38-40, 42, 43, 45, 48, 55, 59, 66, 83, 87, 133

Cowley, Abraham, 122

Creed, John, 41, 58, 114, 143

Crew, John, 25, 34, 134, 135

Cromwell, Oliver, 17, 24, 129

Cromwell, Richard, 17, 24

"Crown" tavern, 40

Cutter of Coleman Street, 122

Davenant, Sir William, 108, 113, 115, 116, 122, 123, 125, 130

Deane, Assistant Master, 36, 85

Dekker, Thomas, 132

Deptford dockyard, 33, 82, 84, 85, 135, 137

"Devil" tavern, 88

Diary (Pepys's), 16-25, 31, 37, 41, 52, 57, 67, 77, 79, 88, 91, 92, 94, 95, 97, 101, 104, 106-9, 112, 114, 118, 123, 126, 128, 130-32, 141, 147, 148-51

"Dog" tavern, 28, 33, 106

Downing, Captain, 104, 105

Drake, Sir Francis, 49

Dryden, John, 115, 117, 120, 127

Duchess of Malfi, The, 113

Edward I, 15

Elborough, Thomas, 98, 142

Epicoene, 119, 121

Epson Wells, 20

Evelyn, John, 104, 150, 151

Evening's Love or The Mock Astrologer, 117

Everyman, 20, 21

Everyman in His Humour, 122

Fairbrother, Dr. William, 81, 93

Faithful Shepherdess, The, 131

Falstaff, 119, 120

Fire, The Great, 19, 88, 110

Fletcher, John, 113, 114, 130, 131

Flora's Vagaries, 128

Index

French Dancing Master, The, 113
Fuller, Dr. Thomas, 98, 100

Gauden, Dennis, 50, 60, 61
Goblins, The, 128
Goddard, Dr., 40, 96
"Green Dragon" tavern, 109
Greenwich, 44, 103, 136, 137
Greeting, Thomas, 109, 110
Gwynn, Ellen (Nell), 86, 126, 128

Hague, The, 25
Hamlet, 18, 118, 121, 124, 125, 131
Hampton Court, 43
Harboard, William, M. P., 149
Harper, Mrs., 74, 90
Harper's Coffeehouse, 90
Harris, Henry, 106, 108, 120, 125
Harvey, Thomas, 40, 47, 96
Hater (Hayter), Tom, 144, 149
Henry IV (Part I), 119, 121
Henry V, 125, 129
Henry VIII, 95
Henry VIII, 116, 119, 120, 121, 131
Heraclius or *The Emperor of the East,*
  116, 123, 127, 131, 132
Hewer, William, 59, 63, 64, 80, 93, 145,
  150
Hill, Thomas, 103, 104, 107
Hinchingbroke House, 69, 74, 94, 97
Hinchingbroke-Montagu-Crew-Carteret
  Clan, 94
Hollyard, Dr. Thomas, 71, 75, 76
Hooke, Dr., 40, 96
Horace, 97
Howard, Lord Henry, 147, 149, 150
"Hudibras," 100
Humorous Lieutenant, The, 123, 124, 126
Hunt, Mr. and Mrs., 67, 90, 107
Hyde Park, 117

Indian Emperor, The, 117
Indian Queen, The, 117, 120, 127
Island Princess, The, 131

Jackson, John, Jr. (the Diarist's nephew
  and heir), 18
Jackson, John, Sr. (the Diarist's brother-
  in-law), 62
Jane (the Diarist's maid), 142, 145, 149
Jonson, Ben, 100, 105, 106, 118, 119, 121,
  130, 131
Joyce, Anthony, 83
Joyce, Mary (wife of Will), 82
Joyce, Will, 52

Katherine of Braganza, King Charles's
  wife, 32, 114
Killigrew, Harry, 84
Killigrew, Thomas, 114, 115, 122, 131, 132
Killigrew, Sir William, 122
King and No King, A, 123
King Arthur, 19, 90
King's College Chapel, Cambridge, 93, 94
"King's Head" tavern, 44, 82
Knights of the Bath, 19
Knight of the Burning Pestle, The, 113

Knipp [Knepp] Mrs., 67, 81, 86, 103-6,
  108, 119, 126, 128
Kynaston, Edward, 125

Lacey, John, 113, 123, 125
Lane, Betty (afterwards Mrs. Martin), 50,
  76, 81-84
Lane, Doll, 84, 85
Laud, William (Archbishop), 20, 89
Law Against Lovers, The, 123
Lawes, Henry, 109
Lincoln's Inns Fields, 118
Love a Cheat (Pepys's unfinished play),
  116
Love and Honour, 113
Love in a Maze, 113
Lovett, the painter, 148
Loyal Subject, The, 125
Luther, Martin, 76

Macbeth, 118, 121, 124
Mad Lover, The, 123
Magdalene College, Cambridge University,
  18, 92, 93, 99
Maiden Queen, The, 117, 126
Maid's Tragedy, The, 127
Martin, Mrs. Betty Lane, 46, 48, 55, 81,
  82-84
Massinger, Philip, 113, 124, 132
Measure for Measure, 121
Mercer, Mary, 86, 87, 102, 103, 106
Merry Wives of Windsor, The, 120, 121
Michell, Betty, 78, 81, 84, 85, 142
Michell (little), Betty's husband, 78, 85
Michell, Mr. (Betty's father), 28, 85, 90,
  142
Michell, Mrs. (Betty's mother), 28
Middleton, Thomas, 130
Midsummer Night's Dream, A, 113, 121
Minnes, Sir John, 36, 66, 137, 138, 139
Moliere, 122
Montagu, Mr. Edward, 32, 97
Montagu, Sir Edward, 17, 24-28, 31-33, 36-
  38, 43, 44, 49, 58, 69, 81, 89-91, 97, 107,
  109, 113, 134, 136, 138-40, 147
Montagu, Lady Jemimah, 20, 24, 32, 67,
  69, 74, 82, 97, 134
Moore, Mr., 58, 144
Moray, Robert, 40, 96
Murford, Captain, 26, 65, 92
Mustapha, 129

Neale, Sir Philip, 40, 96
Newcastle, Duke of, 94, 113
New Theater, 119
Newton, Sir Isaac, 150
Night Walker, The or *The Little Thief,*
  113

"Old Swan" tavern, 85, 142
"Ordinary" tavern, 54
Ormond, James, Duke of, 20, 35, 127
Orrery, Lord, 125, 128
Othello, 121

Palmer, Mrs., *see* Lady Castlemaine
Paradise Lost, 18

Paul's Churchyard, 119

Pembleton, Mr., 67, 70-74

Penn, Margaret, 71, 82, 113

Penn, Sir William, Navy Commissioner, 23, 28-30, 33, 35, 36, 42, 45-48, 73, 86-88, 145, 146

Pepys, Elizabeth (the Diarist's wife), 22, 49, 51, 58, 60, 63, 64-67, 70-86, 113-15, 117, 118, 128, 129, 132, 133, 137, 141, 145, 147

Pepys, John (the Diarist's brother), 16, 62, 78, 85, 92, 93, 97, 98

Pepys, John (the Diarist's father), 16, 62, 63, 68, 70, 78, 85, 90, 92, 93-95

Pepys, Margaret (the Diarist's mother), 62, 69, 70, 78

Pepys, Paulina (the Diarist's sister), 16, 22, 62, 94, 95, 150

Pepys, Robert (the Diarist's uncle), 16, 62, 68, 78

Pepys, Roger, M. P., 47, 62

Pepys, Samuel, son of a London tailor, 15; born in London, 15; mentioned, 15, 16; family relations, 16, 17; reputation with the ladies, 18-36; appointed Commissioner of Tangier, 36; Supervisor of the Chest (pensions), 36-42; Surveyor General of the Victualling, 43-68; gains title to Uncle Robert Pepys's estate, 69-87; attends the Coronation of Charles II, 88-100; practices music, 101-11; goes to the theater, 112-31

Pepys, Thomas (the Diarist's brother), 16, 62, 69, 102

Pepysian Library, 92, 99

Pett, Christopher, 44, 47, 48

Philaster, 123

Plague, The, 19, 88, 103, 133-37, 139-42

Poor Richard (Benjamin Franklin), 21

Popish Plot, 148

Portsmouth Navy Yard, 35

Povy, Thomas, 40, 58, 59, 60, 61, 96

Raleigh, Sir Walter, 49

"Reindeer" tavern, 93, 94

Rivals, The, 123, 125

Rochester, Lord, 127

Romeo and Juliet, 121

"Rose" tavern, 93, 94

Royal Society, 35, 40, 96, 149

Rump (Parliament), 24, 28

St. James's, 36, 46

St. John's College, Cambridge, 93, 94

St. Michel, Balthasar (Balty) (the Diarist's brother-in-law), 149

St. Olave's Church, 71, 101, 147, 150

St. Paul's, 92, 97, 99, 119, 124, 143

St. Thomas's Day, 33, 42

Scornful Lady, 114, 130

Scott, Colonel John, 148, 149

Sedley, Sir Charles, 127, 128

Seething Lane (site of the Navy office and Pepys's lodgings), 28, 60, 64, 65, 133, 143-45, 149

Shadwell, Thomas, 117

Shaftesbury, 148, 150

Shakespeare, 22, 100, 113, 115-21, 131

Shepley, William, 25, 81, 89, 91, 109

Shirley, James, 113, 114, 117, 123, 125

Siege of Rhodes, The, 113, 115

Sir Gawain and the Green Knight, 90

Sir Martin Marall, 94

Slighted Maid, The, 115

Stuart, James, James I, 34

Suckling, Sir John, 128

Sullen Lovers, The, or The Impertinents, 117

"Sun" tavern, 51, 52, 54

Taming of the Shrew, The, 121

Tangier Garrison, 36, 42, 58, 60, 96, 149

Taylor, Captain, 44, 57

Tempest, The, 117, 120, 121

"Three Tuns" tavern, 27

Traitor, The, 125

Trinity College, Cambridge, 92, 93, 94

Trinity House, 96

Tuke, Sir Samuel, 115, 122

Turner, Thomas, 27, 35, 88

Twelfth Night, or What You Will, 115, 120

Unfortunate Lovers, 116

Union, The (ship), 59

Usurper, The, 116

Villain, The, 114, 115

Virgin Martyr, The, 132

Volpone, or The Fox, 122

Waller, Edmund, 42

Warren, Sir William, 30, 50-56

Watts, Isaac, 21

Wayneman, Will, 63, 64

Webster, John, 113

Westminster, 50, 81, 84, 85, 88, 89, 147

Whitehall Palace, 39, 42, 44, 45, 48, 56, 81, 84, 88, 89, 101, 114, 127, 133, 139, 143

Widow, The, 130

Wife for a Month, 114

Wight, Mr. (Uncle Wight), 69, 76, 77, 78

Wild Gallant, 115

Wildgoose Chase, The, 123

William, The (ship), 59

Willett, Deborah (Deb), 64, 79, 80, 93, 94, 117, 118, 128

Wit in a Constable, 113

Wits, The, 130

Woolwich ropeyard, 36, 58, 59, 60, 137, 145

Worse and Worse, 125

Wren, Sir Christopher, 150

Wright, Edith, 77

Wright, Sir Harry, 107

Wright, Lady, 134, 135

Wright, Sir John, 136

York, Duchess of, 127

York, James, Duke of (King Charles's brother), 17, 26, 27, 33-38, 41-46, 48, 54, 89, 96, 101, 118, 119, 127, 133, 134, 143, 147-50